3.5

SHELLS

R. Tucker Abbott, PhD

PORTLAND HOUSE

NEW YORK

This 1989 edition published by Portland House, a division of
dilithium Press, Ltd. distributed by Crown Publishers, Inc.,
225 Park Avenue South, New York, New York 10003

Printed and Bound in Spain

ISBN 0-517-68850-6
hgfedcba

Library of Congress Cataloging in Publication Data

Abbott, R. Tucker (Robert Tucker), 1919–
    Shells / R. Tucker Abbott.
        p.   cm.
    Includes index,
    ISBN 0-517-68850-6
    1. Shells.   I. Title,
    QL403.A225   1989   89-32297
    394′.0471--dc20   CIP

Author: R. Tucker Abbott, Ph.D.
Producer: Solomon M. Skolnick
Designer: Barbara Cohen Aronica
Editor: Madelyn Larsen
Production Coordinator: Ann-Louise Lipman
Picture Researcher: Edward Douglas

For rights information about the photographs in
this book, please contact:

The Image Bank
111 Fifth Avenue, New York, NY 10003

INTRODUCTION

It is said in the land of the Pharaohs that the gods do not subtract from your life span the days that you spend collecting shells, and a few millenniums later Robert Louis Stevenson said it in another way: "It is perhaps a more fortunate destiny to have a taste for collecting shells than to be born a millionaire." It is little surprise, then, that shells have been avidly sought after since prehistoric times, not only for their lasting beauty in shapes and colors, but also as a major source of food, decorative objects, tools and even as a standard form of money.

Man's eternal search for beautiful shells began at the ocean's edge, and today continues in every part of the world. Nearly 80,000 kinds of shells are found not only in the seven seas, but also in most lakes and rivers, as well as high up in the trees of tropical rain forests and in the far corner of most backyards.

With so many areas of the world being threatened by man's destruction of the environment and unbridled pollution, there is a new surge of interest in the living forms in nature, especially in shells made by mollusks.

There are many kinds of "shells," from those that cover eggs and nuts to those that encase crabs and lobsters. Seashells, as we generally know them, are the hard, outer coverings made of lime, or calcium carbonate, secreted by the soft-bodied snails and clams themselves. Members of this shell-producing group, or phylum, are known as mollusks, and unlike other invertebrates (animals without backbones) have a unique organ known as the mantle. This soft, fleshy cape is heavily endowed with glands that secrete the liquid lime and color pigments that finally form the hard, protective shell.

THE LIFE SPAN OF MOLLUSKS

An oyster or clam shell or an empty conch cast up on the beach is merely the end result of a natural life history that began as a microscopic egg, that was joined by a sperm, and that went through many months, or even years, of gradual growth. The shape and coloring of the shell were controlled by inherited genes and modified by its food supply and environmental conditions.

The life span of a living mollusk may vary from a short two years in the case of the edible Bay Scallop, *Argopecten irradians*, to almost a hundred years for a 300-pound Giant Tridacna Clam of the southwest Pacific. The record age for a freshwater Pearly Mussel, raised in an aquarium in Germany, was one hundred years, while the common, edible *escargot* of France may have a longevity of ten years. Most large whelks and conchs found in shallow coastal waters rarely live for more than nine or ten years.

Size is not necessarily an indication of age. Almost three-fourths of all the species of adult shells are less than a half inch in length. In fact, there are several kinds of marine and terrestrial snails that never exceed the size of a grain of rice. Largest and heaviest of the living marine snails is the sluglike Californian Sea Hare, *Aplysia*, which may reach a length of 38 inches and weigh nearly 36 pounds. This animal has a very small, flat internal shell buried under its back. Largest of the shelled snails is the Australian Trumpet, *Syrinx aruanus*, from northern Queensland, which reaches three feet in length. It is a fairly common, intertidal snail whose shell is used by the Aborigines to bail out leaky canoes.

The age of some clams and scallops may be deduced from the darker growth rings, much like those in a cross-section of a tree, although these stoppages in growth, and hence the different color rings, are usually caused by seasonal changes in water temperature. In cold weather growth almost stops and during the warm seasons shell addition may be rapid.

IN SEARCH OF FOOD

Being born is no great problem for most mollusks, but surviving the rigors and dangers of larval and young stages can be a major undertaking. The delicate balance of nature calls for severe culling. If all the offspring from one oyster were to survive, grow to adulthood, and continue to multiply without casualties for ten generations, it would result in a pile of oysters the size of the earth! This is obviously impossible. Fortunately, the food chain in the oceans have been operating for millions of years—the big fish eat the smaller fish, and the smallest fish feed upon yet smaller invertebrates, including the lowly larval forms and eggs of billions of mollusks.

But how do mollusks get their food and sustain themselves with proper diets? The ways are many and perhaps more diverse than in any other phylum. Many are vegetarians, many are carnivores, quite a few are omnivorous with little preference for either plant or animal matter, and some are parasitic on or within other sea creatures. Most bivalves are sedentary, slow-moving filter-feeders, merely straining out microscopic algal diatoms from the sea water, while most snails and squid travel about actively seeking out their animal prey.

RADULAR TEETH

All groups of mollusks, other than the bivalves, possess a feeding organ unique to the phylum—the radula, a siliceous set of tiny teeth arranged on a moveable ribbon that is used as a rasp or licking organ to bite off bits of food. Some snails use the radula to drill holes in other shells. Aristotle was the first to record the action of a radula at work. If you carefully observe a snail crawling up the inside of a glass-walled aquarium, you will see its mouth and radula constantly at work licking at the glass surface. If you hold a hungry land snail or *escargot* in your hand, you may sense or feel it harmlessly attempting to rasp at your skin. Radular teeth are not as hard as glass but are a little harder than a fingernail. Boring through hard shell is augmented by a dissolving fluid made by special glands.

When viewed through the microscope, it was discovered that the radular teeth of snails were very distinct from one group to another. By studying the number or rows, the shape and the ornamentation of the individual teeth, it was possible to build a classification of the marine snails based on radular characteristics. The radula of the pulmonate land snails is correlated with what they feed upon, so that differences in their teeth are not very reliable in identification.

HOW BIVALVES FEED

The lowly bivalves are content to lie buried in the sandy bottom, attached to hard surfaces or anchored by a thread-like byssus (filament) to some submerged object. Food gathering by these sedentary mollusks is accomplished by sucking in food-laden water and passing it over sticky, mucus-laden gills. Microscopic hairs, or cilia, guide the food-laden mucus toward the mouth of the bivalve. Paddlelike soft flaps, called palps, shove and move the diatoms and other bits of vegetable food into the mouth. Undesirable large particles are rejected.

These constantly feeding bivalves are literally filtering the water of their environment, and a colony of clams or freshwater mussels are capable of clearing thousands of gallons of water each day in a relatively small area. The efficiency of these filters depends upon water temperatures, tidal phases, size and number of adult bivalves and the nature of the suspended silt. Over-collecting clams and mussels can have serious consequences on the healthy ecology of a bay or river.

The *Teredo* shipworm, which is a clam and no worm, combines its filter-feeding with a system of specialized digestive tubules to break down some of the wood it bores through. Each year this mollusk causes millions of dollars of damage to wharf pilings and wooden ships. The clam's body resembles that of a long white worm, with a pair of shelly, cup-shaped valves at the boring end. The hole at the surface of the wood is very small and guarded from adverse water conditions by a tiny pair of paddle-shaped pallets. Like most clams, the free-swimming offspring are shed into the open water where they can float away to settle on a new piece of wood. Shipworms are capable of riddling and destroying an entire wharf within a few years. Were it not for the constant, collective action of these "wood-eaters," the ocean would become clogged with floating logs and branches.

In a few deep-sea families of bivalves a carnivorous diet has been developed, mainly because there is apt to be a shortage of algae and chlorophyll in the inky darkness of the ocean depths. Their predatory mode of life includes a system of capturing small crustacea and worms by means of a long, prehensile siphon. In the *Poromya* Dipper Clams the mouth palps may be extended well beyond the edge of the clam, enwrapping the animal prey and dragging it into the mouth.

"MAN-EATING" GIANT CLAMS

There are five species of "man-eating" giant clams, all limited to the shallow, tropical waters of the Indian Ocean and southwest Pacific Ocean. Their flesh is commonly eaten raw or cooked by some of the inhabitants of the South Seas. Their shells are used for making tools and ceremonial figures. In the Solomon Islands the shells have been cut and shaped into large disks and used as money or as symbols of tribal wealth. Pearls from *Tridacna* clams may sometimes reach the size of an orange, and in one instance a large, irregular, or baroque, pearl, known as the Pearl of Allah, grew to a length of 9 inches and a weight of 14 pounds.

The largest of these "killer" or "man-eating" clams is *Tridacna gigas*, which may reach a length of 4 feet, 6 inches, and a weight of dry shell of 507 pounds. No authenticated case is known of a person being trapped or killed, much less eaten, by a giant clam. In fact, all members of this family are vegetarians, obtaining their food in large part by growing colonies of a blue-green algae, *Zooxanthella*, in the upper surfaces of their huge exposed mantle edges. This is the main reason the clams live in shallow water, up-side-down with the hinge of the valves resting on the reef and the wavy, swollen mantle edge facing upwards towards the sunlight. The white blood cells capture the growing algal cells and transport them directly to the digestive gland of the clam. This method of farming algal food occurs in a few other mollusks, such as the *Corculum* Heart Cockle of the Philippines and some small, green, shell-less nudibranch marine snails.

HOW SNAILS FEED

The snails, conchs and whelks have taken on a wide variety of diets, some mollusks being purely vegetarians, others exclusively carnivores, and many being omnivorous. The majority of land-dwelling snails feed on leaves, lichens, mushrooms and, in some cases much to the dismay of farmers, upon seedlings and garden vegetables each spring. European farmers report millions of dollars worth of damage to early crop plantings caused by ground-dwelling snails.

However, most of the large marine snails and whelks are carnivorous, feeding upon other live mollusks or sometimes on sea urchins, starfish, worms, sponges and even small fish. The foot-long *Busycon* whelk of eastern United States seeks out a live hardshell clam, enwraps it in its huge, muscular foot, wedges the edge of its own shell between the valves of the clam and gradually pries them apart. Once a chinklike opening is gained, the snail protrudes its mouthlike proboscis deep into the flesh of the hapless clam. The radula, with its myriad of hooklike teeth, scrapes away at the soft flesh, devouring it completely in an hour or two. A whelk can consume about one clam per week, but the inch-long Oyster Drill, *Urosalpinx*, can destroy a dozen oysters in a few days.

Other meat-eating snails, such as the *Natica* moon snails, bore a hole in the shell of another snail or thin-shelled clam in a matter of hours. Some small, cap-shaped snails, like *Capulus*, that live attached to starfish or scallops all their lives act as parasites and tap the blood system of their hosts. The perfect parasite does not kill the host but keeps draining it of nutrition as long as it can.

THE VENOMOUS CONE SHELLS

While the number of tiny teeth on one radular ribbon may vary from about 100 to 50,000, in some instances they have been greatly modified for very special feeding methods. Cone shells which feed on small, live fish or hunt marine worms in their burrows, have developed long, harpoonlike teeth. Once the single, hollow tooth is plunged into its prey, a very strong venom is quickly pumped through the tooth. This neurotoxin will kill a small goby fish within a few minutes and will paralyze another snail or octopus within an hour. A four-inch-long cone snail can kill and eat a two-inch-long fish, usually one every few weeks.

All 400-or-so species of cones have a harpoonlike set of teeth and all species are doubtlessly venomous, but only six or seven kinds of Indo-Pacific species have been known to kill humans. Two species of Atlantic cones, *Conus regius* and *C. spurius*, have stung people but caused only severe stings. About a dozen human deaths have been recorded, and all of these cases have been in the tropical southwest Pacific, the two worst being from the Textile and the Geography Cones. The related *Terebra* augers and turrid snails also have a similar set of teeth and poison gland, but their only victims are marine worms and their venom is harmless to humans.

Chasing down a moving prey is a problem, of course, for a slow-moving snail, but a few have circumvented this by spending their entire adult lives living within the victim itself. The *Stylifer* Snails live inside the spines of the club-spined sea urchin, sucking the blood of the urchin while maintaining a communication with the outer sea water through a minute opening in the spine. This parasite forms a hollow cyst within the spine, much like that caused by insects in the branches of oak trees. An even more extreme example of internal parasitism exists in a minute snail that lives in the intestine of a sea cucumber, or holothurian. Not until a nineteenth century zoologist examined the anatomy and the radula of this shell-less snail did anyone suspect that this parasite was a snail and not a parasitic worm.

THE GROWTH OF THE SHELL

While the soft parts of a mollusk make normal growth throughout life, including the enlargement of the foot, gills, heart and other organs, the greatest and most obvious expansion takes place in the outer, protective shell. Shell material is produced for three reasons: to have more room to house and support the soft parts; to provide a natural, physiological way of ridding the body of surplus salts, especially calcium; and to serve as a protective armor against predatory crabs and fish.

Turning the intake of food into hard shell material is a complicated process of digestion, assimilation and final deposition—a fundamental procedure common to most animals, and somewhat akin to the creation of fingernails and hair in humans. From special glands located in the mantle, and sometimes in the foot of snails, liquid calcium carbonate, or lime, is exuded and laid down in a hard, crystalized form at the edge or outer lip of the clam or snail. This lime becomes "frozen" in definite, microscopic patterns that may crystalize into aragonite or calcite, the same as one finds in some minerals. Some shelly material may be opaque-white, like alabaster, or may have an iridescent, pearly sheen.

Color pigments are added by nearby glands as the calcium carbonate is laid down. Should the color glands migrate or split into several color centers, a corresponding shift or splitting of the color banding will occur in the shell.

Shell production is greatly influenced by diet, the age of the individual mollusk or by local environmental conditions. A green *Turbo* snail may abruptly produce a white shell, instead of green, if it is fed another species of seaweed. If a *Nucella* dogwinkle lives on a rough, wave-dashed shore, its shell is apt to be smoothish, but its brothers growing in a quiet, inner bay may develop delicate frills and scales. If the water is too acid, especially in the case of shells growing in polluted water, the shell will be very fragile, eroded or not allowed to grow at all.

REPRODUCTION

How mollusks reproduce varies from one family to another. There is no standard system. In most gill-bearing snails, whether they be marine, brackish or freshwater dwellers, the sexes are separate. Usually, the shell and body of the female is larger than that of the males. She has ovaries in the upper part of the whorls and a long, internal oviduct, a tube for the passage of eggs, one by one, to the outside or into an especially made egg-capsule. In the case of the *Trochus* Topshells and the *Haliotis* abalones, as well as most clams, the eggs are shed freely into the water where they may meet free-swimming sperm previously shed by the males. In most cases, however, the eggs are placed in small, protective capsules, usually made of leatherlike, chitinous material and arranged in balls or strands. In some cases, the eggs are covered with a jellylike mass and stuck to weeds, the surface of stones, other shells or, in the case of the *Cyphoma* Flamingo Tongue snails, glued to the branches of sea whips and sea fans. One small freshwater snail, *Oncomelania*, from the Orient covers each egg with her sandy fecal pellets and pats them down into a camouflaged dome.

The common *Busycon* whelks of eastern United States lay long rows of attached disk-shaped capsules, each containing 15 to 50 eggs. Within about four months the eggs mature into miniature replicas of their parents and crawl out through a tiny, round escape hatch. A two-foot-long string may have 150 capsules with a total of 7,000 baby snails. The mortality among newly hatched snails, as well as the young of clams, is enormous because they serve as a main source of food for shrimp, crabs and small fish.

Sometimes several female snails may gather together with a few males and produce a gregarious spawning. In a week they may produce a mound of small capsules the size of a basketball. Occasionally a few male shells may become accidentally covered by new capsules and be trapped for months until the eggs hatch and the capsules break down. Northern Whelks, *Buccinum undatum*, are known to have produced a communal cluster of over 15,000 capsules.

Several factors stimulate sexual activity in mollusks. Sex recognition may be related to the secretion of pheromones—hormonal odors that drift through the water. Female oysters and clams begin egg production as soon as free-swimming sperm trigger a response. Most mollusks spawn at night, but the major factors that start reproduction are temperature changes, salinity levels, moon phases and tidal fluctuations.

The number of eggs produced by one female may vary according to the species. Although *Neptunea* and *Colus* whelks of New England produce about 5,000 eggs per capsule, only one to five of the strongest hatch. The smaller or weaker are eaten by their siblings before they can enter the world. *Natica* Moon Snails lay a sandy collar that may contain up to 11,000 eggs. Cone shells in the Indian Ocean are known to have deposited up to 1,500,000 eggs per female per season.

Laying eggs is one problem, but allowing the young to roam to new feeding grounds or to migrate to other areas is another complication that nature has solved in many ways. Many young mollusks have developed a system of spreading to distant places by going through a free-swimming, larval stage known as the veliger. In some species, the young hatch as miniature replicas of the adults—they literally fall out or crawl out of the egg capsule and proceed "on foot" to new grounds. But most bivalves and many marine snails have a veliger stage—tiny, cilia-(hairlike) covered larval forms that float through the water and may be carried for weeks along with the ocean currents. Young snail veligers born off Yucatan, Mexico, end up in Bermudian waters, and many Bermuda-born veligers may be wafted by oceanic currents to eastern Europe and the Azores.

But even snails that crawl from anchored capsules have a means of distribution. Many capsules are laid on seaweed, the backs of turtles and on bits of floating wood. Even rafts of organ-pipe coral have been found cast ashore, miles from their origin, with egg capsules and young snails embedded in the crevices of the coral mass. A few snails, like the *Planaxis* and *Thiara* gastropods, bear their young within kangaroo-like pouches, either in the oviduct or under the skin of the head, and give birth to perfectly formed, live young.

SEX CHANGES

Some marine mollusks have little respect for the permanence of sex, and, indeed, many regularly practice changing sex from female to male, and sometimes back again. The Eastern Slipper Shell, *Crepidula fornicata*, lives in chains one on top of the other, up to twelve individuals in a pile, with the larger ones at the bottom being female. The top and smaller ones are males. A hormone given off in the water by the females prevents the males from changing sex, but as soon as the females die or are removed, the hormone disappears and the males begin to change into females. The penis shrinks and finally disappears, the shell grows in size, and the male cells in the gonads disappear. When a fully operational female develops, she begins to give off the inhibiting female hormone and all the other slipper shells in the pile return to a fully male status. Sex reversal is not uncommon in *Patella* limpets, *Diodora* keyhole limpets, most wentletraps and a few turrid snails, with a male phase occurring during the first breeding season, but with the functioning female condition existing thereafter.

Oysters, clams and other bivalves are even more ambisexual. Individual oysters may alternate each few months between male and female, a condition known as rhythmical consecutive hermaphroditism. In a large bed of oysters individuals may be in either sexual phase at the same time, so that cross-fertilization is always insured. The quahog, or hardshell clam, *Mercenaria,* may be functioning as a male for the first month, then turn female for the rest of its life.

Most of the air-breathing, pulmonate landshells, such as our garden snails, tropical tree snails and the shell-less slugs are all true hermaphrodites. Both male and female organs are present and functioning in one individual. Two individuals, upon meeting and mating, exchange sperm by means of each other's penis. A few days later each individual lays fertilized eggs, either in the soft earth or wrapped in mucus in a curled-up leaf.

LOCOMOTION

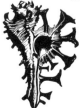

Getting around, whether for short distances to find food, shelter or a better place to reproduce, or whether for long distances for the purpose of expanding the territory of the species, is achieved in many different ways by mollusks. Some do it in a very passive way, depending merely on ocean currents to spread their eggs or larval forms to new areas. Bivalves are the most restricted in their adult travel abilities.

Oysters and *Spondylus* Thorny Oysters are cemented to rocks or shells; *Pinna* pen shells are set deeply in sand; and *Ensis* jackknife clams and the *Teredo* shipworms are trapped in their burrows. As long as ocean currents are bringing food-laden water to its intake siphon, these bivalves have little incentive to move.

Venus clams and the *Mactra* surface clams, however, do make considerable progress by plowing themselves along the sandy bottom. They do this by protruding a flattened, tonguelike foot in front of themselves, swelling up the tip end with blood to form a swollen anchor, and then by pulling themselves forward bit by bit.

MOLLUSKS THAT "FLY"

Fastest of the mollusks are the squids which, by squirting water through their exhalent siphon, can propel themselves backwards at speeds of up to 30 miles per hour. In many cases, especially during a windy night, squid have been known to leap from a wave and, with their lateral fins extended, glide for several hundred feet in midair, much like a flying fish. Although the octopus normally walks about on its eight tentacles, on occasions when it is frightened it will give off a cloud of purple ink and zoom off with a squirt from its siphon and with its eight outstretched tentacles trailing behind.

GLIDING AND POLE-VAULTING ALONG

Snails may glide, hobble along, pole-vault, "inch-worm" or even hop their way through life. The majority glide along by using three functions. First is the production of a mucus slide, a sort of liquid carpet on which to move. This is the silvery trail left after a snail has walked across a sidewalk. Second is the use of microscopic cilia on the underside of the foot that act like paddles. Third is a muscular movement in which waves are created on the underside of the foot that begin at the back and move forward. This action would be akin to your grabbing a small carpet at the back end, giving it a shake to create a wave that moves to the front edge of the carpet and thus moves the whole thing forward by a few inches. Continuous waves in the snail's foot keep it moving forward. An alternative manner is the shuffling of one side and then the other, as in the case of a person in a potato-sack race.

In contrast to the smooth, gliding motion of such gastropods as the garden snail, cowrie or olive shells, is the pole-vaulting of the *Strombus* conchs. The foot of the latter is not broad and flat, but elongate, muscular and bearing a clawlike, horny trapdoor, or operculum, at the end. When the conch wishes to move forward, it extends the foot in front, digs the operculum into the bottom, and pole-vaults forward. These large, lumbering giants, attaining a length of nearly a foot, would find gliding among their native forest of turtlegrass an impossibility.

Surprisingly, the *Strombus* conchs are vegetarians that feed usually on delicate red-brown, soft algae attached to the tough turtlegrass. These docile animals will occasionally flash their clawlike operculum to ward off starfish, crabs and an unwary shell collector. The Fighting Conch of Florida and the West Indies, *Strombus pugilis,* received its scientific name from a European who had never seen a living *pugilis*. He selected the name because the spikes and knobs on the shoulder of the shell resembled those on the metal fighting glove of Roman gladiators.

THE HOMELANDS OF SHELLS

Those who have had a little geography in school are well-aware that the native land of the kangaroos is Australia (and New Guinea), that polar bears are found only in the Arctic (not the Antarctic) and that tigers are limited to southeast Asia. Mollusks, too, have specific and often quite restricted lands where they live. The edible hardshell clam, *Mercenaria*, is found from New Brunswick, Canada, south to the northern half of Florida and over to Texas. Its normal range does not include northern Canada, Bermuda, Europe or the West Indies. Likewise, the lover of warm tropical waters, the Queen or Pink Conch, *Strombus gigas*, ranges from Bermuda and Florida south through the Caribbean to northern Brazil. It is never found in the tropical waters of the Gulf of California or the South Pacific.

Every species of shells lives within its own particular range for several reasons, the main one being its long, geological history, another because the adverse conditions in its bordering lands prevent it from spreading. Most frequently this is due to temperatures that are either too high or too low for the survival of its eggs and young. The absence of especially needed foods or the presence of a very rapacious enemy can also be the controlling factor.

The distribution of marine species is quite different from those of non-marine forms that live on land or in fresh water. The shells of the "seven seas" are, indeed, limited to certain large seas, referred to by students of zoogeography as marine faunal provinces. Largest of these is the Indo-West Pacific, a vast interconnected system of two tropical oceans extending from the Red Sea and East Africa across the Indian Ocean and westward through the East Indies to Polynesia. Hawaii and Easter Island are the easternmost outposts. Such shells as the Money and Snakehead Cowries, *Cypraea moneta* and *caputserpentis*, the *Lambis* Spider Conchs and the *Tridacna* Giant Clams and 10,000 other marine species are limited to this province. The cold waters of South Africa, southern Australia and the northern Japanese islands keep the members of this province from spreading any farther.

Three other unique tropical provinces, mainly kept distinct by bordering continents and major oceanic currents, such as the Gulf Stream, are the Caribbean Province, the Panamanian Province on the Pacific side of Central America, and the West African Province. The latter province, for instance, is unique for its many colorful species of *Marginella* Margin Shells and large *Cymbium* volute shells.

Of course, the extremely cold Arctic and Antarctic regions at the earth's poles have their special molluscan faunas with characteristically drably colored, white shells.

Between these relatively inhospitable cold, ice-strewn provinces and the belt of tropical, equatorial regions are several temperate provinces. Prominent among these in-between regions are the Japanese, Californian and South African Provinces, each with many unique temperate-water species.

Because the thousands of species of land shells, both ground- and tree-dwellers, cannot fly like birds and insects, they usually have very restricted distributions. Just as isolated Australia developed kangaroos and other marsupial mammals, so too did this and other large continents develop unique families and species of land shells. The *Achatina* Giant African Snails were limited to the African continent until man introduced some of them to other lands. Nowhere else do we find *Polygyra* snails other than in North and Central America.

Small islands, isolated and distant from continental influence, became havens for rapidly evolving land snail species. The basic formula for evolution worked efficiently in Hawaii and the South Sea Islands—isolation, genetic mutation and the selection of the best characters for the survival of the new species. Island chains like the Hawaiians and the limestone, isolated mountains of eastern Cuba, blossomed into breeding grounds for hundreds of new species. In some cases, the development of new species along the ridges bordering Hawaiian valleys, took place in a few hundred thousand years.

A similar pattern of distribution developed among the freshwater mollusks, although rarely as sharply defined as in the land species. Today, the mollusks of each major river system are quite distinct. The pearly mussels of the Nile River are quite different from those of the Danube, the Yangtze, the Amazon or the Mississippi. Ancient deep lakes, such as Lake Baikal in the Soviet Union and Lake Tanganyika in Africa each have very curious freshwater snails found nowhere else.

Much to the surprise of exploring naturalists in the early nineteenth century, dozens of new species were discovered in Lake Tanganyika that resembled well-known marine seashells like the nutmegs, terebras and trochids. It was assumed that these were oceanic species descended from forms trapped in fresh water years ago. But later examination of the anatomy proved them to be members of typical freshwater families that had been modified over millions of years because the physical conditions of this huge lake, with its tidal ranges and oceanlike waves, had selected forms best suited to survive in this "inland sea."

SPECIAL NICHES

If one marks a map of an ocean showing the distribution of a marine species, the so-called range of that kind of seashell may extend along the coasts for many thousands of miles. In actuality, the presence of that species may not be continuous and universal, but rather very spotty. This is because the very special environmental conditions required for that species may not be present everywhere. A rock-dwelling species of periwinkle cannot survive along sandy stretches of beaches or in muddy estuaries. Even the preferred sandy bottom for one kind of a clam may differ from another because of the percentage of mud mixture or the average size of the sand grains.

The presence and hence distribution of many mollusks also depends upon the range of a host substrate. In the West Indies, four or five kinds of *Cyphoma* flamingo tongue snails prefer to live only on sea fans and sea whips. Usually only one or two pairs of flamingo tongues will occupy one sea fan. An additional newly-arrived male will soon be chased off the fan by the original, dominant male. These mollusks are obligatory guests, feeding upon the polyps of the sea fan and laying their eggs among its branches.

Perhaps the most popular habitats of shallow water, marine snails are located under slabs of old, dead coral rock. Mollusks are shy, usually nocturnal in habit, and welcome the protection from fish and crabs. A great variety of plant and animal food grows on the underside of these rocks. Considerate shell collector's are aware that sunlight and waves may destroy the eggs and young specimens, so they turn the rocks back as they found them.

THE MYRIAD USES
OF SHELLS

AS FOOD

Early tribes located near the edge of the sea harvested a host of marine animals primarily for food. Archaeological excavations of the kitchen midden, or trash piles, of nearly every primitive human group reveal an abundance of clam, oyster and scallop shells. In some areas, the piles of dead shells became so large that villages and even cemeteries were built upon them. Some inland Indian tribes of North America made freshwater pearly mussels a major part of their diet, especially when game was scarce. Huge piles of these bivalves, some of them extinct today, have been unearthed along the banks of the Ohio and Missouri rivers.

In modern times extensive shore collecting for food mollusks is still carried out daily in many parts of the world, including the South Seas, Africa, the Philippines and East Indies. When a low tide occurs in the evening, people walk the exposed reefs with torches and lanterns in hand to gather live shells and to spear octopus and small fish. This practice has been going on for generations, and it is well that the sea has such regenerative powers.

Almost every kind of mollusk is edible, one of the exceptions being the *Anomia* Jingle Shell, a small bivalve that clings to other shells, crabs and stones. Its raw flesh is extremely acrid, resembling the taste of strong alum. Although mollusks are second to fish and crustacea in the total world poundage fished annually, only about a hundred species of shells are commercially used to any great extent.

Eight of the hundred living species of the oyster family contribute almost a billion pounds of meat each year. Production in some areas has declined dramatically. Landings in the Chesapeake Bay, Maryland, region dropped from 117.4 million pounds of meats in 1880 to 21.2 million pounds in 1965. Today's leading producers are Japan, France and the United States.

Clams have always been a major fishery, for there are

probably about 75 species in various parts of the world that exist in large enough numbers and are in accessible beds to warrant commercial harvesting. The annual catch of the New England Softshell Clam, *Mya arenaria*, varies between 2 and 11 million pounds of meats. The Surf Clam, *Spisula*, used in canned clam chowders, is harvested in eastern United States at a rate of 30 to 50 million pounds. Equally popular is the Hardshell Clam, or Quahog, *Mercenaria*, known in its smaller, younger stage as the "cherrystone." It is harvested by hand extensively from New England to eastern Florida.

The mussel fishery, using several species of the marine family, Mytilidae, is one of the most ancient of the bivalve industries, having been first developed along the coast of France. Millions of pounds are raised on poles, dead branches, suspended ropes or on nets in many tropical and temperate parts of the world.

Squids are a major source of protein for man today, with extensive fisheries being developed in the colder waters of the earth. From 7 to 24 million pounds of the common squid, *Illex illecebrosus*, are landed annually in Newfoundland. Much of it is used for fish bait. Many times this amount of squids are harvested in Japanese waters.

The remaining major worldwide mollusk fisheries include the scallop, the abalones, various conchs, and the extensive cultivation of the edible land snail, or *escargot, Helix pomatia*. Because of the extraordinary and sudden increase in pollution from sewage, city-street run-offs and industrial wastes, the areas where clean and hygienic mollusks may be harvested have been drastically curtailed. To offset this, clam, mussel and oyster rearing began in the 1920's, but did not reach significant proportions until the 1980's. Extensive farming, or the mariculture, of scallops, clams and abalones is being undertaken in Europe, the United States and Japan. Many of the decorative shells and the brightly colored scallops seen in shell shops are "spin-offs" from some of these mariculture ventures.

AS MONEY

It was only natural that the brightly colored, yellow money cowrie, *Cypraea moneta*, would first be used as an ornament for dress, and then later adopted as a major form of currency. Bags of this common and attractive, glossy shell, each about the size of a grape, became a form of money that lasted for over twelve centuries. Their value increased in proportion to the distance from their native source. Chinese and Arabian merchants introduced them to southern China, central Africa and central India long before the birth of Christ. Eventually they became a form of money in the universal business of trading for ivory, rugs and slaves.

The oldest and longest use of the money cowrie existed in India and West Africa, with the main source evidently being the Maldive Islands located south of India. As early as 1346, the Muslim traveller Ibn Battuta records how the cowries were collected and cleaned by the tens of millions and shipped off to Yemen, Thailand and Bengal. By 1515, the Portuguese had taken over the Maldives and had taken control of the "snail trade," as it was called. Eventually the Dutch and then the English took over the trade and by the seventeenth and eighteenth centuries there was a steady flow of tons of cowries through London and Amsterdam to the slave trade in West Africa.

The Germans in the 1850's developed a market for the ringed cowrie, *Cypraea annulus,* which resembled the money cowrie, *C. moneta*. The ringed cowrie had been neglected for years and had become more abundant than its yellow cousin. In ten years, just five German trading companies brought over 35,000 tons of these bright little shells to West Africa, where they were traded for palm oil and then for slaves to be sent to Brazil. It is estimated that 14 billion cowries were collected around the island of Zanzibar in that short period.

The market declined with shell inflation, and by 1896 the last of the great shipments was made from old warehouse stocks in Germany. After 600 years or more of cowrie trading, laws were passed in the African colonies prohibiting their use as money. Small amounts of cowries are still used as money in northwestern Ghana and the Ivory Coast. As late as 1949 it took about 700,000 cowries to purchase a bride in southeast Nigeria.

In Fiji, until a few years ago, the Golden Cowrie, *Cypraea aurantium* was reserved for the use of the village chief, who wore it strung around his neck as a badge of office. In Papua New Guinea large pear oysters are polished and cut into half-moon pendants, called *kina,* and worn around the neck. The modern New Guinea dollar is officially called a kina.

ROYAL PURPLE DYE

Although there must have been many unrecorded expeditions organized in search of money cowries, the first major searches for shells were probably undertaken by the Phoenicians of the ancient Mediterranean world. As early as 1000 B.C. it had been discovered that two species of *Murex* shells found along the coast of the eastern end of the Mediterranean could produce an attractive, permanent cloth dye. It was later dubbed "Royal Tyrian Purple."

The handling of these live snails can produce a bright violet or purple stain on the hands. The agent is a mucus secreted by the gland attached to the inner layer of the snail's soft mantle. For a few minutes the mucus remains whitish to yellow, but with the salt water acting as a mordent, and with the sunlight acting upon the photosensitive liquid, the dye turns purple. Both the Old and New Testaments refer to this ancient dye-making activity.

The story that the dye was discovered because the mouth of a wandering dog had become soaked in purple after the animal had chewed on a live *Murex* shell, and that the appearance of the snails occurred about every seven years, is probably based upon the occasional appearance of the pelagic *Janthina* Purple Sea Snail that also gives off a purple dye.

The *Janthina* snails live in schools on the surface of the ocean and are kept afloat by a raft of air-filled bubbles created by the foot of the snail. Once born, these snails are destined to float a nomadic existence at the mercy of winds and currents for the rest of their lives. Those born and living in the Gulf Stream may be carried as far north as the British Isles. Throughout the world there are four common species, ranging in size from that of a pea to a grape.

Other primitive forays in search of shells were undertaken by the Indians living along the Pacific coast of Central America. Their search in week-long canoe trips was for the *Purpura* Purple Dye Snail that lives along the rocky intertidal zone. Rather than crush and destroy the snails for their dye, as did the Phoenicians, the Indians "milked" their *Purpura* snails into calabash gourds and set the live snails back on the rocks. On their return voyage a week later, the snails were "milked" once again, and the purple liquid put to use in the home village.

IN RITUAL AND RELIGION

As primitive human beings began to think in abstract terms and seek explanations for the natural world about them, it was only natural that shells would be a dominant symbol for their rituals and evolving religions. Shells were already in abundant use as food, ornaments and tools.

Early Neanderthal graves and later paleolithic Cro-Magnon caves of France contained seashells, many placed in mystical patterns around the skulls of the deceased, and others pierced and arranged in belts. Some of the unearthed ivory tusks and reindeer horns had scrimshaw representations of cockle shells and cowries. The presence of Red Sea species, such as the Asellus Cowrie, *Cypraea asellus*, and the Red Helmet Shell, *Cypraecassis rufa*, indicated that these venerated objects had been traded long distances from one tribe of ancient man to the next. Magic, no doubt, was attributed to these beautiful gifts from the sea.

The discovery and adoration associated with nacreous pearls from the Indian Ocean pearl oyster probably gave rise much later to the concept of the birth of Venus from a seashell. If the Mediterranean Greeks and Romans were going to have their goddess of love arise from a bivalve, it certainly was to be the attractive and close-at-hand scallop shell.

The sex cult of Aphrodite, the goddess of physical love, was well established in Greece and Asia Minor by 400 B.C. The early Roman writers, such as the comic dramatist Plautus and later Pliny the Younger, believed that Venus, the Roman equivalent of Aphrodite, was born from a shell. Some claimed that the shell was a cowrie, others insisted it was the scallop shell. The earliest known surviving representation of the goddess of love, portraying her being born from a gaping scallop shell, is a small, terracotta figurine unearthed from a 400 B.C. grave at Taman, on the Black Sea, U.S.S.R. The figure is now in The Hermitage in Leningrad.

Many temples were built for the worshipping of various forms of this love goddess by the Phoenicians, Syrians, Semites and Babylonians. On occasion she is depicted as a protector of sailors. She stood in statue form in a shell grotto in Pompeii with a bronze oar in hand as a symbol of her magical powers to steer sailors to a safe port. Inexpensive, unpainted terra-cotta figurines of Aphrodite, or Venus, emerging from a scallop are quite common in graves of the second and first centuries B.C. The coins of that period, both Phoenician and Greek, bore a replica of seashells, usually of the scallop, *Pecten jacobaeus*.

The ritualistic association of this Mediterranean scallop had a major reawakening in the Roman Catholic Church in Spain in the ninth century. For many centuries prior to this, legend had it that St. James the Apostle was beheaded at the order of Herod Agrippa. The saint's remains, recovered by his disciples, were carried off to Portugal, where through his miraculous intervention, a drowning man and his horse were saved from the sea. Because the horse was found to be festooned with dozens of scallops, the scallop became the insignia of St. James. During the Middle Ages, his shrine at Compostela in Spain attracted Christian pilgrims mainly because Muslims had prevented travel to Jerusalem. Pilgrims returning home to France and England took with them a scallop shell as a memento of their trip to Compostela. The coat of arms of many prominent English families, including that of Anthony Eden, bear scallop shells as witness to their ancestors' pilgrimage to Compostela or participation in the Crusades.

To millions of Hindus in India, the five-inch-long Sacred Chank, *Turbinella pyrum,* has had more meaning and influence that of the scallop among Christians. According to Hindu beliefs, the sacred writings, or Vedas, were stolen by the demon Shankhasura and hidden under the sea in a left-handed specimen of the common chank of India. The God Vishnu plunged into the ocean, defeated the demon, and returned the Vedas to the holy temple. Today, a left-handed chank is always shown in one of the many hands of Vishnu, and is used extensively in religious rites and funeral ceremonies.

Today, this common shell is fished extensively in northeastern Sri Lanka, where huge piles of them bake in the sun waiting to be cut into bangles for sale in temples. Only one in 10,000 or so specimens is left-handed. A good one will sell for about $2,000. There are at least three left-handed specimens in American collections.

Occasionally one may see a left-handed Lightning Whelk from Florida for sale among the roadside stands in India and Sri Lanka with a price tag for this fifty-cent shell exceeding a hundred dollars. Most educated Hindus realize this is not a true sacred chank, but cannot shake off the feeling that its left-handedness has some religious significance.

No shell has been associated more closely with the God of the sea than the triton's Trumpet, *Charonia tritonis*. This is probably because this attractive and capacious shell was one of the first trumpets used by man. Greek mythology relates that during the Great Flood (similar to that described in the Bible), the sea-god Poseidon called upon his son Triton to blow this shell to subdue the floods and quiet the waters. The Romans adopted the legend and the coins of Sicily minted before 400 B.C. show Triton holding his trumpet shell aloft and blowing it.

Curiously, Triton's Trumpet again appears on coins and now postage stamps of South Seas countries because of the belief that this gastropod is capable of eating and controlling the population of the coral-destroying Crown-of-Thorns starfish. In actuality, triton shells normally feed on the smooth, blue or gray Linckia starfish.

A study of the manner in which triton shells are prepared as a horn among various cultures was once made by the Harvard conchologist, Edward S. Morse. He found that half of the world filed off the narrow apex end to form a blow hole, while the rest of the world, including the people in the West Indies, Africa and South Seas, cut a round hole in the side of the spire.

SHELLS AMONG AMERICAN INDIANS

There is a long and interesting history of the use of seashells by almost every group of American Indian, from the Incas and Aztecs of the Andes and the Caribs and Arawaks of the Caribbean to the Pueblo and Huron Indians of the mainland of North America. Shells were used as tools, weapons and liquid holders in Barbados and as sacred containers of spirits of the Athabascan Indians of northern Canada.

Archeologists have retraced trade routes of inland American Indians by identifying the origin of shells found in burial sites. A great trade route existed between the Indian tribes of the Gulf of California and the inland Pueblo Indians. The main kinds were the glossy olive shells and the bittersweet clams, *Glycymeris*. The latter were shaped into frogs and inlaid with small squares of the iridescent, mother-of-pearl from abalone shell.

In the Spiro Mounds made in Oklahoma between A.D. 1200 and 1600 handsome left-handed *Busycon* whelks from the Gulf of Mexico have been excavated, still showing beautiful intricately etched drawings.

Wampum, of course, was a common form of currency and method of recording agreements among the northeastern tribes. Both white and the more valuable purple beads were made from the parts of the quahog, or hardshell clam, *Mercenaria*. It was still used as a form of money among some New England colonists up until the mid-1700's when some overly industrious, mechanically inclined person invented a machine to turn out beads by the millions.

In 1770 British explorer George Vancouver and the settlers who later followed him into the Northwest found that the Indians of British Columbia used the needle-shaped, two-inch-long Precious Tusk Shell, *Dentalium pretiosum*, as a form of money. The shells were strung together in long belts, much the way wampum was done by the Atlantic tribes.

CAMEOS AND SHELL CARVINGS

Shells have been a favored material for the intricate inlays and carvings of many cultures from the Egyptians and early Chinese to the Aztecs and Mayans.

The Chambered Nautilus was a natural candidate for carving and mounting on an elaborate pedestal. Long before nautilus carvings became popular in Europe during the Renaissance, the Chinese of the Ming Dynasty had already been producing detailed dragon scenes in the pearlized surface of the nautilus shell. The most famous nautilus carvings were produced by three generations of the Bellekin family. The original carver was Jeremie Belquin, a maker of inlay ornaments for muskets and pistols. He moved in the mid-1500's from Metz to Amsterdam, and passed on his knowledge to his son and then to his grandson, Cornelius (now Bellekin). His carved and signed nautilus goblets were the rage of eighteenth century European courts.

Although some carving was already a fine art during ancient Roman times, it was not done on shells but on mineral gems, such as onyx, sardonyx and carnelian. The use of shells, with their differently colored layers, did not come into use in Europe until the fifteenth century. Artists first used small cowries to fashion cameos for small rings. This gave the cameo a lighter, upper layer and several darker, lower areas of brown or purple. Earliest of these ring makers was Benvenuto Cellini, who set up his operations in Rome in 1519.

By that time, a steady supply of the large helmet shells was reaching Italy—the Bull-mouth Red Helmet, mainly from Zanzibar, the Emperor's Helmet from the West Indies, and to a lesser extent the Queen Conch, *Strombus gigas*, from the Caribbean. The very common Horned Helmet, *Cassis cornuta*, from the East Indies was not suitable for cameos because it had a reputation for "doubling," that is, the middle of white layer would part from the lower orange color.

A school of cameo shell carvers began to develop in Trapani, Sicily. Some of the camerists, as they were called, ventured to London and Amsterdam. By the eighteenth century, Naples and its suburb Torro del Greco became the leading cameo-carving center. In 1810, there were 200 families working on cameos. In addition to the small, oval "garbo" cameos, cut from the shell and mounted on silver pins and clasps, there was a huge market for large, exquisite mythological scenes left intact on the shell. In 1878, there were 80 cameo cutters in Rome and 30 in Genoa. The trade spread to Paris, where eventually there were more than 3,000 French camerists at work making inexpensive, mass-produced shell carvings. About this time, thousands of convicts from France were banished to New Caledonia, among them evidently men trained in shell carving, resulting in a flood of carved nautilus shells that appeared on the market in the late 1800's.

The death knell of the great cameo carvers was at hand with this overproduction in Paris and New Caledonia. The final blow came after World War I when plastic replicas and imitation ceramic cameos came on the world market. The glorious depictions of the elopement of Helen with Paris, the triumph of Bacchus, and of Mazeppa, tied on the horse and hunted by the wolves of the forest, are now relegated to the cabinets of the great art museums.

PEARLS

As almost everyone knows, pearls are the result of an irritating sand grain accidently lodged in the flesh of a pearl oyster and subsequently being covered over, layer by layer, with nacreous shell material or so-called mother-of-pearl. This is only partially true, because all shelled mollusks, including conchs, garden snails and all bivalves are capable of producing a pearl. The causes of the irritation may be the intrusion of almost any small object, whether it be a sand grain, a microscopic parasite, an egg of a marine creature, a shrimp or even a small fish. The protective mantle will cover the foreign body with layers of mother-of-pearl.

The size, color and shape of a pearl may be determined by the location of the foreign body. A pearl developing in a Pink Conch of the West Indies will be a beautiful, glossy pink color. A pearl lodged along the black edge of a clam or oyster will be black. The Giant Tridacna Clam, whose interior shell is alabaster white, will sometimes form a white, spherical pearl the size of a golf ball.

The commercial, iridescent gem pearl comes from one of several species of *Pinctada* pearl oysters. The native pearl of Sri Lanka comes from a pearl oyster the size of a small dinner plate, while the species used in Japan for cultured pearls is much thinner and the size of a saucer. Other pearl-producing oysters grow well in the lower Caribbean, around Isla Margarita (the word *margarita* means "pearl"), the Gulf of California and the Society Islands in French Polynesia.

Not all pearls are perfectly spherical. Many are misshapen or attached to the side of the oyster shell. These are known as baroque pearls, which have less value and are usually mounted in settings that hide the blemished side. Baroque pearls are commonly found in freshwater pearly mussels and sometimes in the beautifully iridescent abalone shells of California. The largest known pearl, a 14-pound baroque monster with a crude white finish, came from a Giant Tridacna Clam. The legendary and illusive "coconut pearl," sought in vain for centuries, did not come from a coconut, but was actually a pearl from this giant clam.

Those who shuck clams and oysters at a commercial "raw bar" usually find several pearls during a day's work. The value of these pearls is very low, since they have the same color and finish as the bivalve that produced them. Rarely, a perfect, spherical, purple pearl the size of a pea, is found in a hardshell or cherrystone clam and will bring a few dollars.

The popularity of pink pearls from the Bahamian conchs and the coffee-colored pearls from the freshwater unionid mussels of rivers waxes and wanes through the years. The so-called Queen Pearl from a New Jersey river mussel was sold in the nineteenth century to Empress Eugenie of France for $25,000. The pink conch pearls may sell for a hundred to several thousand dollars, depending upon perfection and size, but purchasers should be aware that these pearls will inevitably fade to white, especially if exposed to sunlight.

THE ROMANCE OF SHELLS

THE EARLIEST COLLECTIONS

That pretty shells were appreciated and perhaps venerated by early man is attested to by the presence of Tiger Cowries and the Bull-mouth Red Helmet shell in the graves of Cro-Magnon man. Much later, a few centuries before Christ, shells were collected as curiosities and assembled systematically in formal collections. When the ruins of Pompeii in Italy were carefully excavated, a large collection of shells was unearthed. Many of the specimens collected before the eruption of Vesuvius in A.D. 79 had evidently come from the Red Sea and the Persian Gulf. Even in those days shells were being brought home from far away lands. Pliny the Elder, the great Roman historian, lived in Pompeii and was president of the natural history society in that ill-fated city. It is quite possible that the unearthed collection had belonged to him or to the society.

A nineteenth century Italian malacologist reported the presence of the Angular Triton, *Cymatium angulatum,* in the Pompeii collection. Either this is a misidentification of this common West Indian species, or, indeed, proof that some European voyages to the West Indies had occurred long before those of Columbus.

THE FIRST BOOKS ON SHELLS

Gradually, the mania for shell collecting spread throughout Europe after the fall of the Roman Empire. Illuminated medieval manuscripts, the work of monks in monasteries, commonly bore excellent pictures of Indian Ocean shells. Not long after the development of the printing press, books by Conrad Gesner in 1553 and Ole Worm in 1655 carried woodblock engravings of Asian and African shells.

The great age of early sea voyages opened up new collecting grounds as the Dutch, French, Danes, Spanish and English sailed in search of new lands, minerals, spices, rare woods and medicinal plants. Naturalists and sailors on Columbus's voyages brought back landshells and seashells from Cuba, Hispaniola and the smaller Caribbean Islands. Not long afterwards, these mollusks were illustrated in color in magnificent zoological books.

The earliest book devoted solely to mollusks was produced by the Italian naturalist Fabio Colonna in 1616. In it he wrote about his own observations and illustrated for the first time such shells from West Africa as the Elephant Snout Volute, *Cymbium*, and the Costate Cockle, *Cardium costata*, from Angola. The first "textbook" on shells was written by the Jesuit priest Philippo Buonanni in Rome in 1681. He aptly entitled his work, "Recreation of the Eyes and the Mind through the Observation of Shells." Despite some of the curious notions current in that day, he copied the best from the works of Aristotle and Pliny, and extolled the virtues of shell collecting. Many of the species he illustrated came from the West Indies and the Indian Ocean.

EARLY SHELL COLLECTORS

Physicians, because of their training in biology and interest in the curiosities of life, have had a great influence on the science of conchology, or malacology, as some call it. Earliest of these was Martin Lister, physician to Queen Anne of England, and forebear of the physician of the same name, after whom the mouthwash, Listerine, is named. He began his writings on mollusks in 1669, and with the help of his two daughters produced a huge tome with many thousands of woodcut engravings that appeared at intervals from 1685 to 1692. Botanists and fur hunters exploring the New World for treasures brought back a flood of new and interesting shells which fell into Lister's hands.

Perhaps the greatest of the early conchologists was Georg Rumphius, a Dutch accountant and naturalist sent in 1650 by the Dutch East India Company to Amboina on Java Island. During his many years of residence in Indonesia he collected, made personal observations on and described thousands of forms of shells and other marine life. He produced a huge illustrated manuscript, including many, very large wood engraving blocks, which he entitled

"Cabinet of Amboina Curiosities." Everything was sent off by ship to Holland, but a storm overtook and sank it. The undaunted Rumphius toiled another dozen years to duplicate his masterpiece, but went blind before he could finish. His Indonesian wife and his assistants completed the task, with Rumphius "proofing" the woodblock engravings by touch. He died before the book was finally published in Holland in 1705.

When Carl Linnaeus, the Swedish naturalist, wrote the tenth edition of his famous 1758 *Systema Naturae* and described some 700 species of shells in a book that was to start the practical system of applying a genus and species name to each species, the illustrations from these books of Rumphius, Buonanni and Lister were used in place of lengthy descriptions. Thus the "binominal," or two-name system was born.

HUGH CUMING, THE GREATEST COLLECTOR
Of even greater impact was the prodigious collecting activities of the Englishman Hugh Cuming, born in Devon in 1791. As a young boy he was tutored and instilled with a passion for shells by Col. George Montagu, a prominent writer on English mollusks. Hugh was apprenticed to a sailmaker and upon learning the trade, he first settled in Buenos Aires and later in Valparaiso, Chile. By the age of thirty-five he had amassed a fortune and retired to spend the rest of his life collecting shells. His activities as the world's foremost shell dealer made it possible for him to maintain his wealth.

Cuming personally collected and assembled through exchange the largest collection of shells ever brought together by one man. It is estimated that his collection contained 19,000 species, an enormous number for the day, when it was bequeathed to the British Museum in 1866. It is likely that he must have collected over 5 million specimens during his lifetime. He was the first to design and outfit a yacht, the *Discoverer,* for the sole purpose of collecting and storing shells. He set sail on October 28, 1827 for the Polynesian islands and during the first voyage of eight months he visited many islands, including Easter, Pitcairn, Tahiti and the Marquesas. In 69 days he and his divers collected 28,000 pearls, most of which, however had a small value.

At Pitcairn Island he had the assistance of John Adams, the last survivor of the nine *Bounty* mutineers who had taken refuge from Captain Bligh. Curiously, and perhaps ironically, Captain Bligh also collected shells, and his wife's famous collection was put up for auction in London five years before Cuming's first voyage. The widow's shell cabinet was made of wood obtained from the captain at Botany Bay, Australia, a famous shell collecting spot.

Hugh Cuming's second voyage was along the coast of South and Central America, as far north as the sea of Cortez, Mexico. He dredged extensively along the way, obtaining hundreds of new species later to be described by such famous conchologists as Sowerby, Reeve and Philippi. In Central America, the Indians showed him how to extract the Royal Tyrian Purple dye from the *Purpura* rock snails by pressing the snail's trapdoor. The skein of cotton dyed by him in May 1829 is still preserved in the British Museum (Natural History).

Cuming returned to England in 1831 with his freshly collected shells and soon became the darling of the English collectors and shell book writers. Sowerby's beautiful work, *The Conchological Illustrations* published from 1832 to 1841, contains 200 hand-painted, steel-engraved plates, illustrating most of Cuming's newly discovered species.

But Cuming, now in his mid-forties, was still vigorous and anxious to return to new tropical collecting grounds. The then unexploited Philippine Islands with its tantalizing sampling of exotic marine shells and gorgeous tree snails was a lure he could not resist. Armed with ambassadorial documents and an ability to speak fluent Spanish, Cuming descended upon almost every major island in the archipelago, enlisting the aid of Catholic priests, hundreds of native divers and thousands of school children. The shells rolled in almost faster than he could clean and pack them. It is estimated that he discovered about 3,000 new species of Philippine mollusks, most of them terrestrial and freshwater, but many marine in origin. From 1827 to 1850 one genus and over 105 new species were named after Cuming. Another 92 had been named *cumingii* or *cumingiana* by 1870, and there are still new species being given his name today. His record of finding new species of plants is equally impressive.

EUROPEAN VOYAGES FOR SHELLS
At last the stage was set for modern expeditions for shells. For centuries specimens had dribbled back into the marketplace of Europe or directly to wealthy nobles and merchants who vied with each other for Neptune's treasures. The wealthy English apothecary James Petiver wrote a pamphlet in the late 1600's on how sailors should collect and preserve shells. Sir Hans Sloane, a physician and an early governor of Jamaica, assembled a West Indian shell collection that was later to be the nucleus of the natural history collection of the British Museum.

The earliest and most significant of the great nationally-sponsored voyages were the three commanded by Capt. James Cook. In 1768 the British Government commissioned Cook to proceed to the South Seas to observe the transit of Venus across the sun's disc. Aboard were two prominent naturalists, Sir Joseph Banks, then twenty-five years of age and not yet knighted, and Dr. Daniel Solander, a former Swedish pupil of Linnaeus. These transformed the *Endeavour* into a floating museum of natural history before it returned to England in 1771. During the three voyages, including the last during which Cook lost his life in Hawaii, many hundreds of new species were collected and ultimately reached the shell collections of prominent English conchologists.

The greatest expedition mounted by the British Government was the voyage of the biological research vessel, *Challenger*, which explored the deepest known parts of the Atlantic and Pacific oceans from December 1872 to May 1876, a voyage which covered a distance of 69,000 nautical miles and made 362 dredging stations. About 1,800 species of mollusks were collected, some from depths of 2,900 fathoms, over three miles down.

The British sponsored many other scientific voyages over the years, but mollusks played a small part in the research. A few species, including several new barnacles, were collected by Charles Darwin on the voyage of H.M.S. *Beagle* in 1832 to 1836 to the Galapagos Islands. On the exploring voyage of the *Samarang*, from 1843 to 1846 to Indonesia and eastern Asia, the ship's surgeon, Dr. Arther Adams, collected and later described many new species, some of which had come up in the bottom mud adhering to the ship's anchor. Adams put his catch in dishes of sea water and made beautiful paintings of the live animals that were later published in 1850.

AMERICAN VOYAGES FOR SHELLS
Not to be outdone by the expanding ventures of the European nations, young America at the urging of its scientists· organized the U. S. Exploring Expedition in 1837 to chart the South Seas and make a survey for new whaling stations. A young Boston seaman and naturalist, Joseph Pitty Couthouy, travelled to Washington, D.C., and personally persuaded President Andrew Jackson to intervene on his behalf to have him made the Conchologist of the Scientific Corps. The expedition set out in 1838 from Norfolk, Virginia, rounded Cape Horn, and made numerous stops throughout the Polynesian Islands. Because of a quarrel with the commanding officer, Couthouy left the expedition in Samoa.

The collections from the voyage were placed in the basement of the then-new Smithsonian Institution. A minister and amateur naturalist volunteered to care for the shells, which at first had been carefully preserved in jars of alcohol. Thinking that the small, tin labels bearing the precious station numbers were staining the specimens, the volunteer removed them and carefully placed them in a separate jar. Despite the loss of the locality data, a creditable report was eventually prepared by the Boston conchologist, Augustus A. Gould.

RARE SHELLS

In nature there are probably no truly rare shells, that is, so unique and represented by so few specimens in the wild that they may be considered scarce. Unlike manmade stamps and coins which are sometimes known only from a single misprint or a few surviving examples, shells are living creatures that readily reproduce. Most of the high-priced "rarities," such as the $14,000 Fulton's Cowrie or the $5,000 Rumphius Slit Shell, are probably relatively common in their natural habitat. Unfortunately for collectors, they live at considerable depths or in inaccessible locations under sea cliffs, so that few specimens have come to light. Most of the several dozen specimens of the 1½-inch Fulton's Cowrie have been collected, not by divers or with nets, but from the stomachs of the Mussel Cracker fish off the coast of Natal, South Africa. The snail-eating fish swallows a cowrie, then grabs the bait and hook of a deep-water fisherman, and is

brought to the surface and degutted before the digestive juices in the stomach can do damage to the beautiful, glossy surface of the shell.

To rank as a choice, desirable collector's item a shell must be rare in collections, difficult to obtain in good condition, be large and beautiful enough in color or sculpturing to be admired and the envy of other collectors. It helps if there is a fanciful story or history associated with the species. There are many small, drab species, known only from one or two specimens, that would bring only a few dollars on the open market. Shells that were once considered rare and choice a few hundred years ago and once went at public auctions for huge sums are now worth but a few dollars. New collecting methods or the happy discovery of their optimum habitat made them easily obtained. In short, the market was flooded with some species. That is one reason why the mariculture of certain rare shells would not only be very expensive but also impractical in the long run.

Perhaps the most famous of the rare shells that has fallen from its exalted status as the "world's rarest shell" is the Glory-of-the-Seas Cone, a five-inch moderately attractive shell with graceful outlines and numerous fine, tentlike markings. The first specimen turned up in a Dutchman's collection in 1757. Even at that early date cone shells were the favorites of most European shell collectors. Friedrich Chemnitz, a naturalist of Nuremberg, Germany, described and christened it in 1777 as *Conus gloriamaris*, the Glory-of-the-Seas, and for eighty years that specimen was the envy and Holy Grail of all shell collectors. By 1827 only four other specimens had turned up, but still no one knew where it lived, other than somewhere in the South Pacific.

The shell world was electrified in 1836 at the news that the well-known collector, Hugh Cuming, had found two live specimens under a rock on a reef on Bohol Island in the Philippines. "I nearly fainted with delight," he reported. To add to the momentous occasion, the English writer S. P. Woodward invented two untrue stories, the first that three, not two, specimens had been found, and that an earthquake had engulfed and sunk the reef soon after Cuming's find. Thus, the only known locality for this species had disappeared forever!

To add to the mystique of this species, Woodward told another unsubstantiated story of the French collector, already owning the only known specimen in France, outbid every rival at a shell auction to obtain the second known specimen. Having won the cone, he crushed it beneath his heel, explaining, "Now my specimen is the only one!"

By 1954, 26 specimens of the Glory-of-the-Seas had been found, most of them in the Philippines and Indonesia at well-documented localities. Yet it still remained the most sought-after species. In 1963, several good examples turned up in the British Solomon Islands. A 5½-inch specimen was purchased for $2,000 and presented to the Academy of Natural Sciences of Philadelphia. Scuba divers in the Solomons, normally occupied in recovering brass propellers and other salable objects from warships sunk in World War II, turned their searches to rare cones and cowries. Off Lunga Point on the north coast of Guadalcanal Island came dozens of specimens from a depth of 90 feet, and more recently in the southern Philippines tangle nets have brought up over two hundred specimens. By 1980 the bubble had burst and some good specimens were selling for less than a hundred dollars.

Other cones that have experienced a similar fall from grace are the Matchless Cone, *Conus cedonulli*, of the lower Caribbean, the St. Thomas Cone, *Conus thomae*, from Indonesia and Thailand, the Rhododendron Cone, *Conus adamsonii*, from central Polynesia, and the Palisade Cone, *Conus cervus*, from the Philippines. All once sold for $1,000 or more apiece, but now all may be obtained for one fifth the price. Waiting in the wings to become more available are such rarities as Vic Wee's and Du Savel's Cones.

Among the early priceless treasures was the Precious Wentletrap, *Epitonium scalare*, which appeared in the best of the Dutch collections as early as 1663. During the next 150 years it commanded a very high price at auctions. The two-inch, pure-white shell with exquisite, thin, erect ribs is a handsome example of nature's architectural abilities. The first few specimens came from the East Indies. It is reported that a French duchess exchanged a country estate for a perfect specimen, and that Maria Theresa's husband, Kaiser Franz I Stephen, paid 4,000 guilders for one about 1750. By the early 1800's it was still bringing large sums in London. However, the species is relatively common in northeastern Australia, so not long after the settlement of that continent prices began to tumble, and today one may be purchased for a few dollars.

S. P. Woodward again invented a story that Chinese merchants had manufactured forgeries from rice-starch paste. There is some doubt that this could be done successfully, and for years collectors have sought in vain for one of these genuine counterfeits. If found, it would be worth one hundred times the value of a real one!

The history of rare shells has intrigued amateurs and scientists alike, so much so that the English conchologist, S. Peter Dance, devoted an entire book to the subject (*Rare Shells,* University of California Press, Berkeley, 1969). He presented a fascinating account of the fifty rarest shells, some of which today are considered fairly common. Twenty years later, only ten would still be considered rare, but another forty new ones could be added.

Outstanding in value today among the exalted are the two-inch Fulton's Cowrie from South Africa, Broderip's Cowrie from off Mozambique, and the Charleston Slit Shell, *Perotrochus charlestonensis* Askew, the latter described as recently as 1988. It was recovered 90 miles east of Charleston, South Carolina, in 650 feet of water by the submersible, *Johnson-Sea-Link I*. Well-known in the fossil record of 300 million years ago, the genus was considered extinct until a live one was discovered in the West Indies in 1856. This genus of primitive snails is characterized by a long, natural slit in the last whorl. To date, with new collecting methods at the disposal of conchologists, twenty-five new species and subspecies have been discovered. A large specimen of Rumphius's Slit Shell, almost the size of a basketball, was recently dredged off Taiwan and purchased for $6,000 by an Italian shell collector.

FAKES AND FREAKS

Many shells brought up freshly from the sea are either covered with a natural, brown covering, or periostracum, or may sometimes be heavily encrusted with algae, coral or sponges. Soaking the shell in a strong alkali, scrubbing, picking away with a steel probe and boiling the shell to remove the meat were the standard methods used for years. Sometimes collectors and dealers gave their shells a face-lifting by chemical treatment, although by the eighteenth century the practice of using acid was universally condemned because this gave an artificial, oily appearance to the surface.

Rumphius stated in his 1705 *Amboinsche Rariteikamer* that "in order to keep their vivid lustre one must immerse them in seawater now and then, say every two years. This is called dunking the shells. After this they may be rinsed in fresh water, dried in the sun [in the shade would be better], rubbing them long and gently with a woolen cloth, until they get warm and will shine like a mirror [cowries and olives, evidently]."

The doctoring of shells was extensively practiced among Dutch dealers in the 1700's. Chipped lips were carefully filed smooth, unsightly cracks and holes cleverly sealed over, lost spines ingeniously replaced, and faded spots rejuvenated with paint. In the collection at Harvard's Museum of Comparative Zoology is the only known specimen of a pink Paper Nautilus, *Argonauta argo*, which is the parchmentlike, normally white, egg case manufactured by an octopuslike creature. The owner paid $1,000 for it about 1850. A hundred years later, tests showed that the specimen had been artificially dyed.

Occasionally one finds in old collections specimens of strangely spotted and streaked tree snails from the Philippines. These specimens of *Helicostyla* tree snails, of which there are about 150 varieties, are greatly sought-after by connoisseurs of terrestrial shells. A French dealer of the nineteenth century altered the color pattern of the outside of the shell by applying a hot iron. In 1987 a popular German book on tropical land snails illustrated two of these fakes in the belief that they might be new species.

Altered specimens are nothing new. Carl Linnaeus, the earliest to name new species, was duped himself by a highly polished Arabian Cowrie. The surface of the shell had been ground down to reveal the violet-colored layers below. He named it *Cypraea amethystea* in 1758 after the amethyst and believing it a new species. This same kind of buffing was commonly done to other small cowries and shipped into China for use as currency. Early Chinese accounts refer to small, "rubbed" purple cowries—not truly purple ones like the rare *Cypraea poraria*, but merely polished *Cypraea annulus* and *caputserpentis*.

NATURAL FREAKS

It is not surprising that with most mollusks being capable of producing hundreds, thousands and, in some cases, tens of thousands of offspring in one season that nature should produce many abnormal specimens. Freaks may be caused by a genetic mutation, an error in the early divisions of the egg, physical injury to the shell-making mantle or even unfavorable environmental conditions.

The most common cause of freaks is physical injury to the edge of the mantle. Hermit crabs and bottom fish break away parts of the shell-producing mantle and may stop the growth of spines, create double spines or change the direction of growth of subsequent whorls, thus causing the spire to "lean over." On rare occasions a large hole may be punched in the last whorl, through which the animal may protrude and begin another new aperture. If injury is done to the lip of a shell, it is usually soon repaired. Rarely, one may find a Melo Volute from Australia with distinct, saw-tooth scars caused by a shark bite.

Most snails are coiled dextrally, that is, the shell coils clockwise as new shell material is added by the mantle to the edge of the lip. (If a viewer holds the snail shell with the narrow apex pointing up, the opening, or aperture, will be on the right). Very rarely, a mutation or injury in the developing egg will cause the shell to grow counterclockwise, or sinistrally. These "left-handed" freaks are extremely rare in some species, especially the cones, cowries and murex shells. In the glossy, little *Marginella* Margin Shells left-handed specimens are not rare, occurring perhaps one in a ten thousand specimens. A few kinds of seashells, such as Florida' Lightning Whelk, are normally left-handed. A right-handed specimen is a collector's dream come true. Especially rare and choice is a left-handed Junonia, *Scaphella junonia,* only four having been found in the last two hundred years.

Albinism is not uncommon in some species but unknown in others. Usually pure-white specimens exhibit albinism in the shell but not in the soft parts. In southwest Florida, albino Egmont Cockles, *Trachycardium egmontianum,* and the Florida Crown Conch, *Melongena corona,* are not very rare, but seldom found. Pure black specimens of olives and cowries are quite rare in most, but not all, species of these glossy shells.

Even Mother Nature has attempted with great success to create false shells, the commonest being the caddis fly larval case. The case is build of minute grains of quartz sand cemented into a coiled tube. These larval fly cases have been mistakenly described as new mollusk species on three different occasions. Equally astounding is the two-inch-long worm tube of cemented sand grains produced by the polychaete marine worms, *Pectinaria.*

TODAY'S GREAT SHELL COLLECTIONS

Throughout the world there are about 30,000 serious shell collectors banded together in over 100 shell clubs. There are several national associations, with two in the United States: the American Malacological Union, for professional conchologists and students of mollusks; and the Conchologists of America, a society for over 1,000 amateur hobbyists.

Great private collections exist in the United States, Japan, Italy, Germany, England and Australia, most of them specializing in shells of their own country, but many are cosmopolitan. Some collections are renowned because of their self-collected nature, others are well known because their owners acquired a nearly complete collection in certain families through exchange and purchase.

Largest and most complete of the shell collections in the United States, and perhaps in the world, is that housed in the Division of Mollusks of the U. S. Natural History Museum under the Smithsonian Institution in Washington, D.C. Their research collection, not on view to the public and kept in dust-proof cabinets, is so immense that only a fraction of it can be put on display. By 1989, it had 980,00 separate lots, or samples, of shells, each lot accompanied by a data slip with locality, date of collecting, and the collector's name. Each specimen is carefully numbered to prevent mixture. Another 100,000 lots await cataloging. The collection may have as many as ten million specimens. Four scientists, all trained conchologists, are continually carrying out research in connection with the collections. It is believed that the national collection has about 30,000 species, about one-third of the known kinds.

The second most important and the oldest active scientific collection of mollusks is in the Academy of Natural Sciences of Philadelphia, which was founded in 1812. It is about half the size of the national collection but is particularly rich in type specimens—the shells that were actually used when the species was first described and named by America's pioneers in conchology: Thomas Say, Isaac Lea, Timothy Conrad and Henry A. Pilsbry.

Other equally important museum collections of almost the same size are found at Harvard's Museum of Comparative Zoology in Cambridge, Massachusetts, the American Museum of Natural History in New York City, in Chicago's Field Museum of Natural History, and in the California Academy of Sciences in San Francisco. Other large collections are located in Los Angeles, Gainesville, Florida, San Diego, Honolulu, Houston and Pittsburg.

The only museum solely devoted to amateurs and schools is The Shell Museum and Educational Foundation on Sanibel Island, west Florida. This newly developing institution, located on America's best-known collecting beaches, is devoted to the dispersal of knowledge about mollusks through exhibits, seminars and publications.

Outside the United States, there are large, important, scientific collections, usually supported by the government. The most prestigious and one of the oldest is that of the British Museum of Natural History on Cromwell Road, London. Their excellent exhibits and great, historical collections are unrivaled. Other major centers of molluscan studies are in Paris, Berlin, Frankfurt-am-Main, Brussels, Leiden, Copenhagen, Sydney, Auckland, Tokyo and Ottawa.

OPPOSITE: Like gifts from the sea, this array of clams and cockles expresses nature's variety of shapes and colors.

Eight shelly plates, bounded by a muscular girdle of tiny beads, characterize the polyplacophoran class of mollusks. Unlike snails, they lack true eyes and tentacles. The **West Indian Chiton** is common on shore rocks. (*Chiton tuberculatus* Linnaeus, 1758. 2.5 in./6cm)

A cluster of inch-long **Coquina Clams** thrust out their delicate, tubelike siphons to breathe in fresh seawater. Class: Bivalvia. (*Donax variabilis* Say, 1822. 1 in./2.5cm)

The lumbering, foot-long **Florida Horse Conch** is a carnivorous member of the gastropod, or univalve, class of mollusks. (*Pleuroploca gigantea* (Kiener, 1840) 30cm)

Rarest of the five known kinds of Chambered Nautiluses is the **Umbilicate Nautilus** from Papua New Guinea. Like the octopus and squid, it belongs to the cephalopod class. (*Nautilus scrobiculatus* Lightfoot, 1786. 8 in./20cm)

FOLLOWING PAGE: Colorful scallop shells.

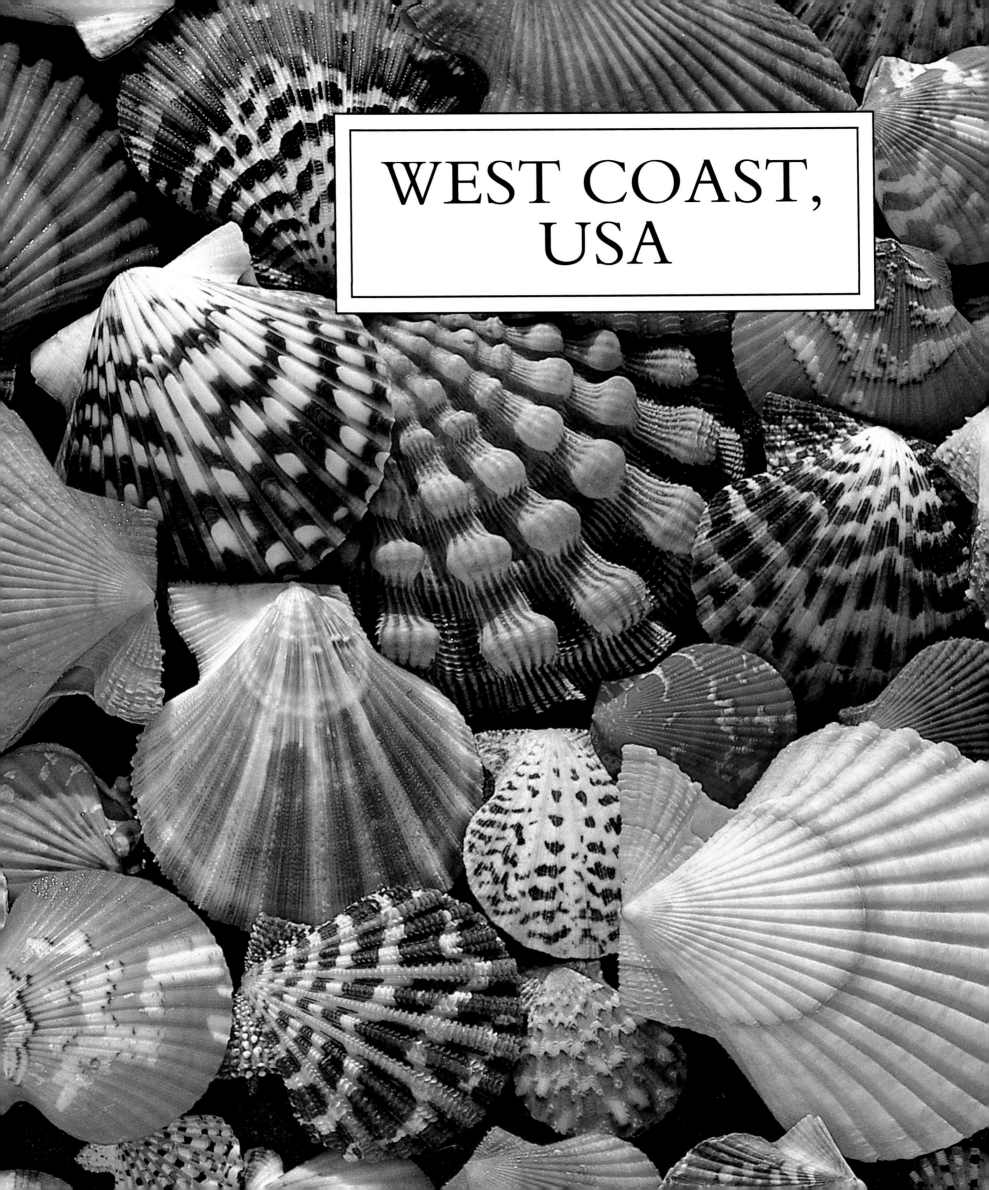

WEST COAST, USA

Among the enemies of oysters in California is the 1.5-inch **Poulson's Dwarf Triton,** a common dweller of rocks at the low-tide mark (*Ocenebra poulsoni* (Carpenter, 1864). 4cm)

The rocky coasts of California abound with limpets, some of which have a natural hole at the peak of the shell. The inch-long **Volcano Limpet** grazes on moss and seaweeds at night. (*Fissurella volcano* Reeve, 1849. 2.5cm)

Living on the long kelp weeds of southern California in 100 feet of water the **Norris Shell** feeds on vegetable matter. Its operculum, or trapdoor, is round and soft and can seal off the opening of the shell. (*Norrisia norrisi* (Sowerby, 1838). 2 in./5cm)

Of the dozen kinds of top shells found along the Pacific coast of North America, the inch-long **Ringed Top** is the most beautiful and most commonly found among kelp beds. *Calliostoma annulatum* (Lightfoot, 1786). 2.5cm)

The Pacific coast of North America has a varied assortment of many hundred kinds of shells, from the drably colored inhabitants of the cold waters of Alaska to the brightly colored cowries and trivia shells of southern California. Many species of clams and snails live offshore well below the ocean's surface.

Recently adopted as the official state shell of Oregon, the 4-inch fuzz-covered **Oregon Triton** lives offshore from the Bering Sea to northern California. (*Fusitriton oregonense* (Redfield, 1848). 10cm)

Scarcely a half-inch in size, the well-ribbed **California Trivia** was formed by the snail's enveloping, fleshy mantle. In southern California and Mexico it is common under the intertidal rocks. (*Trivia californiana* (Gray, 1827). 1cm)

To children's delight, the **Spiny Cup-and-Saucer** shell is occasionally cast up on the beach from southern California to Chile. It lives on rocks and other shells. (*Crucibulum spinosum* (Sowerby, 1824))

Eight shelly valves bound together by a leathery girdle characterize this **Lined Red Chiton,** a member of the small Polyplacophora class of mollusks. (*Tonicella lineata* (Wood, 1815). 1 in./2.5 cm)

The **Leafy Thorn Purpura** of the Pacific coast bears a sharp prong at the edge of the lower lip which it uses to pry open barnacles and mussels. (*Ceratostoma foliatum* (Gmelin, 1791)). This rock-dweller grows to 3 inches (8cm) in length.

ABOVE: This delicately frilled mussel-eater, familiarly known to California rocky shore collectors as the **Three-winged Murex,** is a common 2-inch collector's item (*Pteropurpura trialata* (Sowerby, 1834). 5cm)

The magnificent coastline of western United States stretches for many hundreds of miles from the peaceful waters of Puget Sound to the wave-dashed, rocky shores of the Big Sur country of central California. A thousand ecological havens support over a thousand species of shelled mollusks in the shallow, cool waters of the Eastern Pacific.

FOLLOWING PAGE: bivalves sport many colors and shapes.

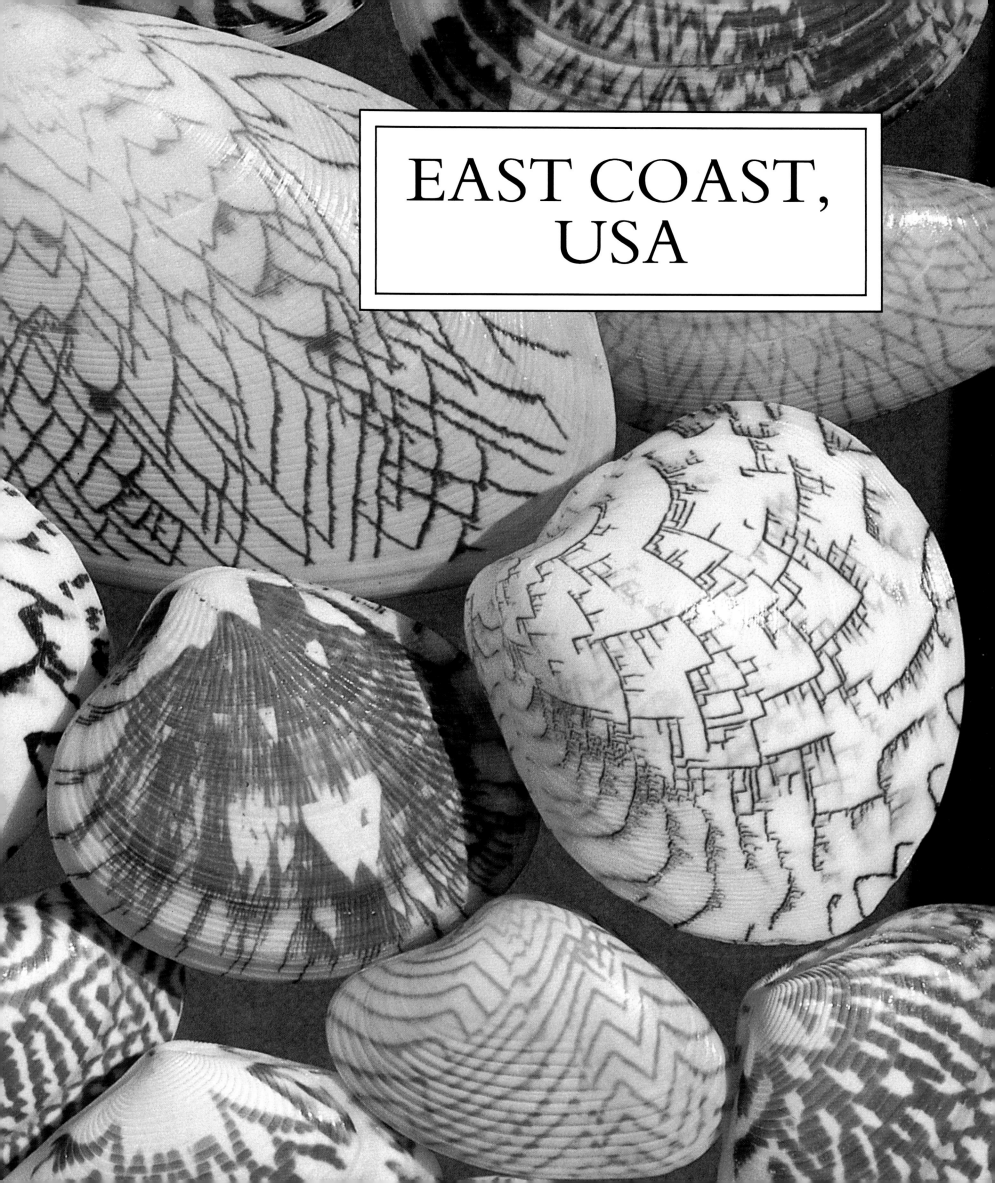

EAST COAST, USA

Beau's Murex is the only Florida and West Indian murex with such extensive webbing between the spines. This uncommon, deep-water snail feeds on small bivalves. (*Siratus beauii* (Fischer and Bernardi, 1857). 4 in./10 cm)

Swarms of the **Virgin Nerite** each 1/3-inch in size, may litter the muddy weed flats of West Indian islands and the lower Florida Keys. (*Neritina virginea* (Linneaus, 1758). 1cm)

The triton family has many small members, including this common **Gold-mouthed Hairy Triton** from the coral reefs of southern Florida. (*Cymatium nicobaricum Röding,* 1798). 2 in./5cm)

Like rockets bursting under water, the **American Thorny Oysters** spread their orange and yellow spines out for protection. In nature they may be camouflaged with sponge and weed growths. (*Spondylus americanus* Hermann, 1781. 4 in./10cm)

The abundant and voracious **Common Crown Conch** of Florida is always on the prowl for small tree oysters and delicate bivalves. (*Melongena corona* (Gmelin, 1791) 2 in./5cm). Also called the *King's Crown*.

All along the mangrove tree areas of the Gulf of Mexico, from Florida to Yucatan, Mexico, the **Common Crown Conch** displays a variety of shapes and bandings. (2 in./5cm)

Only very lucky shell collectors ever find a ***Junonia*** cast up on a Sanibel Island beach in Florida. This 4-inch beauty from the volute family has been treasured by conchologists for hundreds of years. (*Scaphella junonia* (Lamarck, 1804). 10cm)

Scallops can swim by quickly snapping together their shelly valves. Here a **Calico Scallop** peers out with its many tiny blue eyes. Inside is the edible, round muscle. (*Argopecten gibbus* (Linnaeus, 1758). 2 in./5cm)

Surprisingly lightweight for its size, the **Atlantic Partridge Tun** has a large open shell to accommodate the huge animal which feeds on starfish. (*Tonna maculosa* (Dillwyn, 1817). 4 in./10cm)

Its foot armed with a sickle-shaped claw, the **Florida Fighting Conch** can ward off marauding crabs and fish. At the tip of the tentacles are colorful eyeballs. (*Strombus alatus* (Gmelin, 1791). 3 in./8cm)

Normally brick-red in color, the **Lion's Paw Scallop** from southeastern United States is rarely all yellow or even albinistic. Its meat is edible, but the shell more treasured by collectors. (*Lyropecten nodosus* (Linnaeus, 1758). 5 in./12cm)

The venus clam family has over a hundred species, most coming from shallow, sand-bottomed bays in warm-water countries. Large swollen ridges mark this inch-long **Imperial Venus** from southeastern United States. (*Chione latilirata* (Conrad, 1841). 2.5cm)

With its valves shut tight, the **Lion's Paw Scallop** from Florida cannot reveal its row of many tiny, brown eyes along its fleshy mantle edge. The shell may grow 6 inches across, with the knobs sometimes containing seawater. (*Lyropecten nodosus* (Linnaeus, 1758). 15cm)

Since prehistoric times, the foot-long triton shell has been used by man as a trumpet and was always associated in ancient sculptures and paintings with the sea god, Triton. The **Atlantic Triton's Trumpet** is from the West Indies and Mediterranean. (*Charonia variegata* (Lamarck, 1816). 30cm)

Related to the scallops, this 2-inch **Spiny Lima** can swim by flapping its shelly valves and waving its long sticky tentacles. It is also capable of building a nest with its spiderlike byssal threads. (*Lima lima* (Linnaeus, 1758) from southeast Florida. 5cm)

The cold-water lover **New England Neptune** lives offshore feeding on clams and blue mussels. It ranges from the Arctic Seas south to New York. (*Neptunea lyrata* subspecies *decemcostata* (Say, 1826). 3 in./8cm)

The eastern shores of North America extend from the icy waters of Labrador through the cold, rock-bound areas of New England, southward to the semitropical sand beaches and coral reefs of the Florida Keys. Tidepools, marshy inlets, sand dunes, muddy bays and broken coral rock offer a wide choice of habitats for nearly 2,000 marine species of shells of the western Atlantic.
Bar Harbor, Maine, is a collector's delight at the beach at ebb tide.

Not infrequently cast up on the beaches of west Florida is the lightweight **Common Fig Shell,** a dweller of sandy bottoms. It has no operculum, or trapdoor, attached to its foot like the ones in many other kinds of snails. (*Ficus communis* (Röding, 1798). 3 in./8cm)

The predatory **Banded Tulip** of southeastern United States will attack and eat almost any other snail and demolish it within an hour. It also feeds on bivalves, such as the oyster and clam. (*Fasciolaria lilium* subspecies *hunteria* (Perry, 1811). 3 in./8cm)

While alive, the **Atlantic Hairy Triton** has a natural, protective covering of periostracal hairs. When cleaned, this tropical shell reveals its minutely beaded sculpturing. (*Cymatium pileare* (Linnaeus, 1758) from Florida and the West Indies. 3 in./8cm)

The gnarled and constricted aperture of the **Atlantic Distorsio** is presumably to protect the animal from hungry hermit crabs. It is common in 30 to 80 feet of water in southeastern Florida. (*Distorsio clathrata* (Lamarck, 1816). 2 in./5cm)

Along a deserted beach in New Jersey a pair of **Atlantic Surf Clams** await an appreciative shell collector. Millions of these offshore clams are annually fished and processed into fried clams or clam chowders. (*Spisula solidissima* (Dillwyn, 1817). 4 in./10cm)

In most tropical parts of the world along rocky coasts the family of small, toothed nerites are present. They scrape away at algae growths at night. The **Four-toothed Nerite** is common in Florida and the West Indies. (*Nerita versicolor* (Gmelin, 1791). 3/4 in./2cm)

Although more at home in the eelgrass beds of the West Indies, the 6-inch *True Tulip* is occasionally found in southeastern United States shallow waters. (*Fasciolaria tulipa* (Linnaeus, 1758). 15cm)

Symbol of the Bahamian kingdom of the seashell, the **Pink** or **Queen Conch** has served as an ornament, trumpet and source of food for centuries, both in Florida and the West Indies. (*Strombus gigas* Linnaeus, 1758. 8 in./20cm)

This nondescript, white snail resembles a crumpled hat. The **White Hoof-shell** adheres to other shells and breeds its small eggs under its foot. (*Antisabia antiquata* (Linnaeus, 1758). Florida Keys. 1 in./2.5cm)

Denizens of green eelgrass beds of the Lower Florida Keys, these common, 2-inch **Long-spined Star-shells** have a small, white shelly operculum, or trapdoor, to seal out enemies. (*Astraea phoebia* (Röding, 1798). 5cm)

Best known of the large marine shells of southeastern United States is the "left-handed" **Lightning Whelk.** These are 4-inch juveniles, but when foot-long adults, they lose their streaks and become solid white. (*Busycon contrarium* (Conrad, 1840). 10cm)

The long, many-whorled **Flame Auger** is an uncommon, offshore sand dweller of southeast Florida and the West Indies. It feeds on marine worms. (*Terebra taurina* (Lightfoot, 1786). 5 in./12cm)

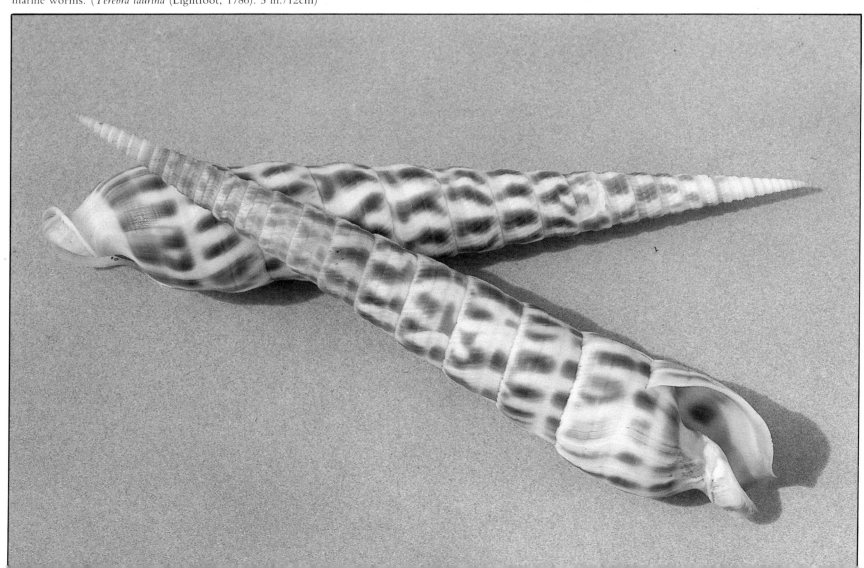

Although not rare, the 5-inch **Angular Triton** of southern Florida and the West Indies is difficult to find among the dense eelgrass beds where it feeds on clams. (*Cymatium femorale* (Linnaeus, 1758). 12cm)

FOLLOWING PAGE: The pea-sized **Emerald Nerite** of southeast Florida and the West Indies is commonly used in shell jewelry (0.5cm).

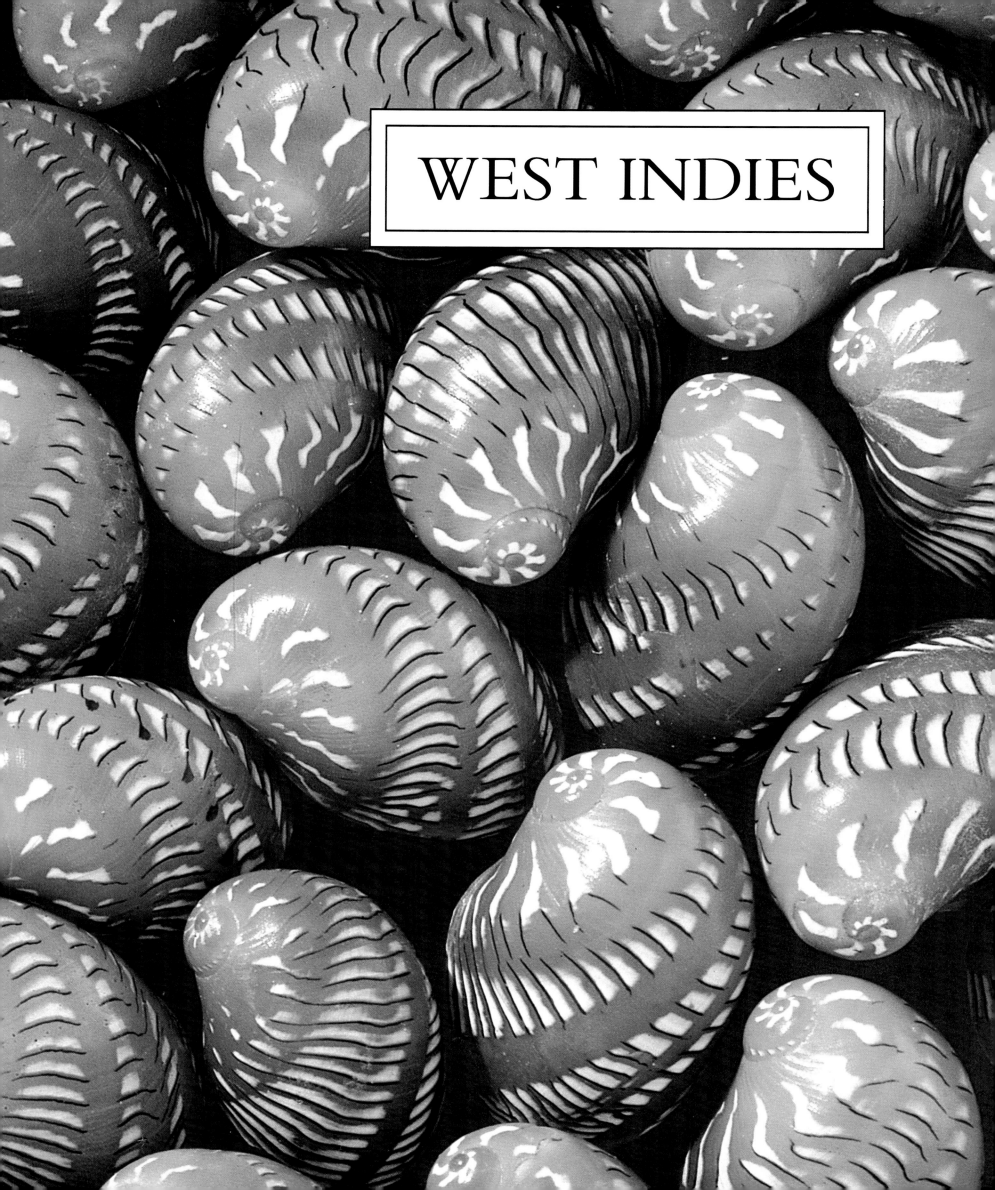

WEST INDIES

The Caribbean Province is a warm-water region inhabited by marine life unique to its ecological conditions. Stretching from northern Brazil, through the Caribbean basin, and northward to the Florida Keys and Bermuda, it supports such tropical shells as the Emerald Nerite, Pink Conch, Latirus Shells and Bleeding Tooth Nerite.
The Turk and Caicos Islands off the north coast of Haiti are typical of the warm shallow seas of the Bahamian archipelago.

The family of spindle-shaped latirus and tulip shells has many ornately colored species, including this 2-inch **Trochlear Latirus** from Haiti. (*Latirus cariniferus* (Lamarck, 1816). 5cm)

A graceful outline and dainty beads mark **Springer's Top** shell, a deep-water treasure from a depth of 1,600 feet in Caribbean waters. (*Calliostoma springeri* Clench and Turner, 1960. 1.5 in./4cm)

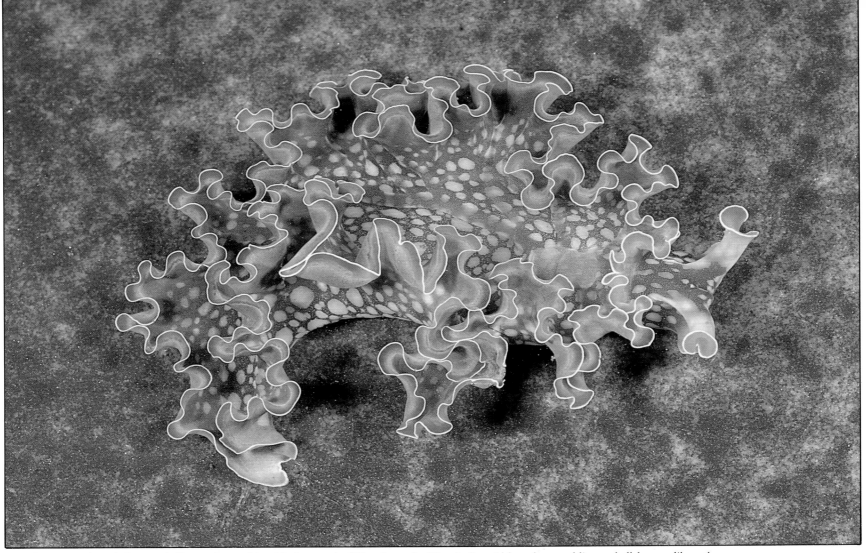

Not all gastropod snails have a shell, as witnessed by this **Lettuce-leaf Slug** from the West Indies. Although resembling a shell-less nudibranch snail, it is actually related to the seahares, *Aplysia. (Tridachia crispata* (Mörch, 1863). 2 in./5cm)

The choicest collector's items of the Caribbean are the deep-water slit shells of the family Pleurotomariidae. Newly discovered in 1988 is the very rare, 4-inch **Charleston Slit Shell, Pleurotomaria (Perotrochus)** *charlestonensis* Agnew. A live one is seen here among sponge beds in 600 feet of water (10cm).

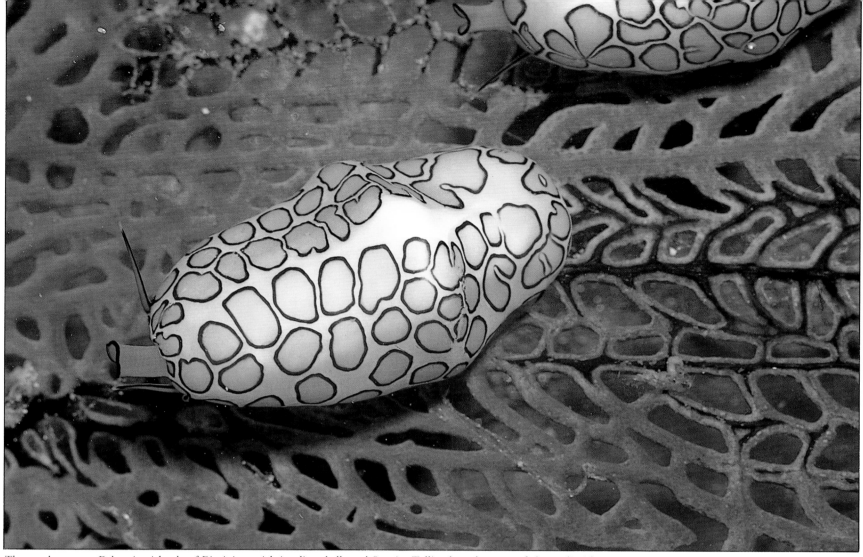

The northernmost Bahamian islands of Bimini are rich in olive shells and Sunrise Tellin clams because of almost limitless stretches of clean, white sand. Pictured here is the **Flamingo Tongue** commonly found living on sea fans. (*Cyphoma gibossum* (Linnaeus, 1758). 1 in./2.5cm)

Limited to the large high islands of the Greater and Lesser Antilles is the **West Indian Crown Conch** which prefers the muddy sands near mangrove trees. (*Melongena melongena* (Linnaeus, 1758). 4 in./10cm)

No West Indian shell has endeared itself to children more than the **Bleeding Tooth Nerite,** so common along the rocky tide line. The shelly operculum, or trapdoor, is smooth and reddish brown. (*Nerita peloronta* (Linnaeus, 1758). 1 in./ 2.5cm)

Three sharp folds on the inner lip of the **West Indian Chank** characterize the family of chank and vase shells. In life, this common, shallow-water shell is covered with a natural, brown outer "skin." (*Turbinella angulata* (Lightfoot, 1786). 8 in./20 cm)

This curious, inch-long glossy shell belongs to a family of parasitic snails. The **Dolabrate Pyram** is a sand-dweller and lives both in the tropical Atlantic as well as in the southwestern Pacific. (*Pyramidella dolabrata* (Linnaeus, 1758). 2.5cm)

Among the choice West Indian murex shells is this **Spectral Murex,** living on deep reefs and rarely collected. Only scuba divers are likely to find them. (*Chicoreus spectrum* (Reeve, 1846). 4 in./10cm)

The bars and notes on the surface of this Caribbean species inspired the name of *Voluta musica* (Linnaeus, 1758). The **Music Volute** lives in shallow, sandy areas and eats dead marine organisms. 3 in./8cm)

The 2-inch long **Rough Lima** clam from the West Indies keeps its shelly valves together with the help of a small black pad, or *resilium,* in the hinge. Like the Spiny Lima (p.41) the animal has long tentacles. (*Lima scabra* (Born, 1778) 5cm)

FOLLOWING PAGE: Limpets come in many forms (1.5 in./4cm).

MEDITERRANEAN

The edible **Oxheart Clam** has a wide distribution from Norway to the Mediterranean and a great range of depth from 24 to 9,000 feet. (*Glossus humanus* (Linnaeus, 1758). 3 in./8cm)

Eaten by the ancients and today by the people of the northern Mediterranean, the beautifully ribbed **Hians Cockle** was also an inspiration to artists. (*Ringicardium hians* (Brocchi, 1814). 3 in./8cm)

FOLLOWING PAGE: The Asturias Coast of Spain.

St. James's Scallop became a badge of honor and symbol for the Christians of the Middle Ages, as well as being a great delicacy for the table. (*Pecten maximus* subspecies *jacobaeus* (Linnaeus, 1758). Mediterranean. 5 in./12cm)

The well-sculptured **Mediterranean Bark Triton** lives offshore in the Cape Verde Islands and throughout the Mediterranean Sea. (*Cabestana cutacea* (Linnaeus, 1767). 3 in./8cm)

OPPOSITE: Giant Tun. 10 in./25cm (*Tonna galea* (Linnaeus, 1758)).

71

PRECEEDING PAGES: The marine shells of the Canary Islands, far to the west of northern Africa, are mainly Mediterranean in origin, but also have a strong affinity with those of the West African marine province. Isolated Tenerife Island, shown here, has a few unique endemic species of shells.

The **Common Pelican's-foot** has been a part of shell collections since Roman times, and today is seen in shops and roadside shell stands throughout Europe. (*Aporrhais pespelecani* (Linnaeus, 1758). 2 in./5cm)

FOLLOWING PAGES: An array of clams and cockles.

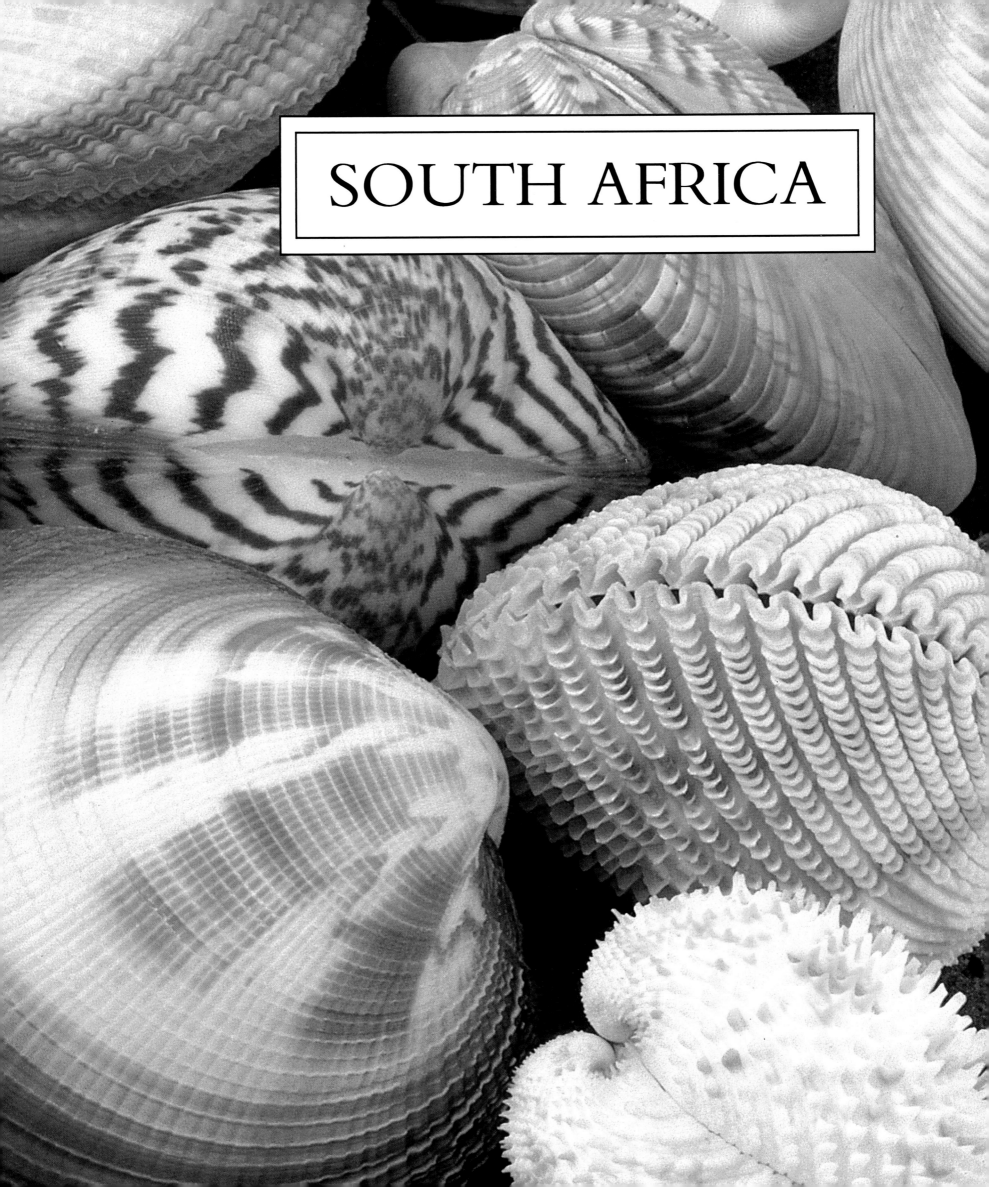

SOUTH AFRICA

Discovered in 1897, **Gilchrist's Volute** of cold South African waters remained a collector's rarity until deep-sea trawlers discovered their beds in the 1960's. (*Neptuneopsis gilchristi* (Sowerby, 1898). 7 in./18cm)

OPPOSITE PAGE: Limpets abound on the rocky shores of the Cape Peninsula in South Africa.

The interior of the abalone shells sparkles with reflective, iridescent colors. Four species of this snail family inhabit the rocky shores, just below the wave-line, in South Africa. (*Haliotis* species. 3 in./8cm)

Worldwide in tropical and semitropical waters are the sturdy Turban shells, many of which have characteristic, hard shelly opercula, or trapdoors, to protect the inner animal. (*Turbo* species. 3 in./8cm)

Unlike its cousin, the **Common Pelican's-foot** of Europe (p. 74), the **African Pelican's-foot** bears long, slender prongs on its outer lip. (*Aporrhais pesgallinae* Barnard, 1963. Southwest Africa. 2 in./5cm)

Also related to a European triton (p. 70) is the **Ridged African Triton** from fairly deep water along the coast of South Africa. (*Cabestana dolarium* (Linnaeus, 1767). 3 in./ 8cm)

The **South African Turban** is normally a dull-colored shell, but when polished, it glistens with the colors of Jacob's coat.
(*Turbo sarmaticus* Linnaeus, 1758. 3 in./8cm)

Like ancient ships at sea, the Argonauta, or **Paper Nautilus,** has intrigued shell collectors with an insatiable wandering lust for foreign shells. (*Argonauta argo* Linnaeus 1758. South Africa. 8 in./20cm)

The *Paper Nautilus* is not a shell in the true sense, but the parchmentlike egg cradle of the Argonaut, a pelagic member of the octopus clan. Two of the female's flattened tentacles secrete the egg case.

OPPOSITE PAGE: When originally described in 1947, this stunning deep-water shell from South Africa was thought to be a volute, but subsequent anatomical studies of the animal proved it to be a giant marginella shell. **Pringle's Marginella** is now classified as *Afrivoluta pringlei* Tomlin, 1947. 3 in./8cm.

This family of deep-sea slit shells was thought to be long-extinct until a live one was found in 1855. Now sixteen species are known, including the very rare **African Slit Shell,** showing its round, horny operculum in the aperture. (*Pleurotomania africana* Tomlin, 1948. South Africa. 5 in./ 12cm)

Many strange new species are being discovered today in northeastern Africa, but well-known since 1811 is the much sought-after **Festive Volute** that lives in deep water of Somalia. (*Festilyria festiva* (Lamarck, 1811). 5 in./12cm)

Considered the most valuable shell in the world during the 1980's, several specimens of **Fulton's Cowrie** have each sold for more than $10,000. Most are recovered from the stomach of the Mussel Cracker fish of South Africa. (*Cypraea fultoni* Sowerby, 1903. 2.5 in./6cm)

The rocky, wave-dashed seashores of South Africa abound in a variety of limpets. Commonest in some places is the **Long-ribbed Limpet,** a nighttime vegetarian. (*Patella longicosta* Lamarck, 1819. 2.5 in./6cm)

FOLLOWING PAGE: **Calf Moon Snail.** Indian Ocean. (*Natica vitellus* Linnaeus, 1758. 1.5 in./4cm)

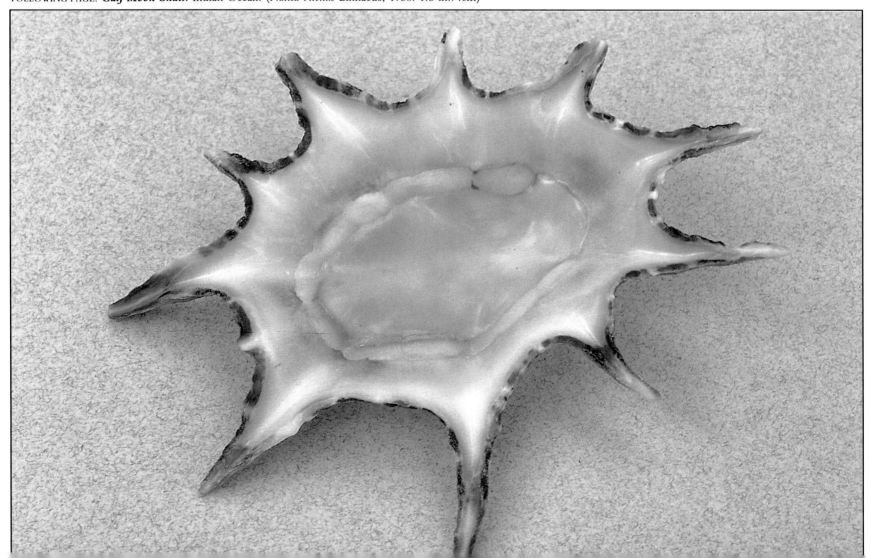

INDIAN OCEAN

Widely distributed in the Indian Ocean and southwest Pacific, the lightweight, large **Spotted Tun** is one of a dozen members of this family. (*Tonna dolium* Linnaeus, 1758. 4 in./10cm)

BELOW: Of all Indian Ocean shells, only the **Violet Spider Conch** displays a deep violet throat. This desirable species commands a high price among collectors. (*Lambis violacea* (Swainson, 1821). Mauritius. 3.5 in./9cm)

OPPOSITE PAGE: The Seychelle Islands in the Indian Ocean harbor many strange shells.

The chunky **Black-spotted Triton,** common on reefs throughout the Indo–West Pacific Province, is characterized by the two black squares on the inner lip of the mouth. (*Cymatium lotorium* (Linnaeus; 1758). 3.5 in./9cm)

Choicest of the Indonesian cones is the 2-inch **Victor Cone,** a lost species rediscovered by a German shell collector, Renate Wittig, in the 1980's. (*Conus nobilis* subspecies *victor* Broderip, 1842. Bali. 5cm)

Most of the world's species of volutes have been located and classified, but in 1985 the rare **Clover's Lyria** was discovered in Sri Lanka and named after a well-known American shell dealer. (*Lyria cloveriana* Weaver, 1963. 3 in./8cm)

Rarely exceeding a foot in length, the **Fluted Giant Clam** of the tropical Pacific and Indian Oceans is sometimes called the "furbelow clam" because of its wavy yellow and orange frills. (*Tridacna squamosa* Lamarck 1819. 30cm)

For centuries, Arabs distributed these two common kinds of Maldive Islands cowries as a form of standard currency: the yellow **Money Cowrie** and the **Gold-ringer Cowrie** (*Cypraea moneta* Linnaeus, 1758 and *C. annulus* Linnaeus, 1758. Both 1 in./2.5cm)

The Maldive Islands lie in the center of the tropical Indian Ocean south of the Indian continent. For 600 years they have been a major source of cowrie shells used for trade and money in Asia and Africa. Today they supply a vast amount of the "tourist shells" seen in shell and gift shops all over the world.

Closely related to the *Strombus* conchs, the common **Chiragra Spider Conch** is a vegetarian living in shallow-water coral reefs of the Indo-Pacific region. The spread-out "fingers" prevent the shell from being rolled over by waves. *Lambis chiragra* (Linnaeus, 1758). 6 in./15cm)

Like a vaulted cathedral, the **Cock's-comb Oyster** creates a dramatic outline as it grows to the sides of wharf pilings in the southwest Pacific; although edible, very little meat is contained between the valves. (*Lopha cristagalli* (Linnaeus, 1758). 4 in./10cm)

For years, the many-ribbed **Imperial Harp Shell** was known only from a few specimens. Its homeland is in the vicinity of Mauritius in the southwestern part of the Indian Ocean. (*Harpa costata* (Linnaeus, 1758). 3 in./7.5cm)

Usually hidden under dead coral blocks, the small **Strawberry Goblet** of the Indian Ocean is a tiny jewel once it is cleaned of its outer periostracal skin. (*Pollia fragaria* (Wood, 1828). 1 in./2.5cm)

As this shell meticulously creates its circles of tiny brown ridges, it accents their ends by forming brown beads on the white outer lip. The **Lesser Girdled Triton** is less than two inches in size (5cm). *Gelagna succincta* (Linnaeus, 1771). South Pacific.)

Nearly all of the hundred kinds of murex shells create rows or varices of long, protective spines, but the **Rose-branch Murex** paints the tips a beautiful rose. *Chicoreus palmarosae* (Lamarck, 1822). Sri Lanka. 4 in./10cm)

Known only from the Sultanate of Oman in southern Arabia, this exquisite little shell was recently discovered by an American medical missionary and named after his wife, Eloise. **Eloise's Bubble Shell** is fairly common on the reef flats of Misira Island. (*Acteon eloisae* Abbott, 1973. 1 in./2.5cm)

The sea god's trumpet is represented in the Indian and Western Pacific oceans by the **Pacific Trumpet Triton**. It is distinguished from its Atlantic brother (p. 40) by the wide, cream streaks on the inner lip. (*Charonia tritonis* (Linnaeus, 1758). 13 in./32cm)

The commonest and most widely distributed of the spider conchs in the Indo-West Pacific is the **Common Spider Conch.** The spines, developed only at maturity, of the females are usually longer and more strongly curved. (*Lambis lambis* (Linnaeus, 1758). 4 in./10cm)

FOLLOWING PAGE: **Pheasant Shells** from southern Australia. *Phasianella australis* (Gmelin, 1791). 2 in./5cm)

AUSTRALIA

Australia is the land of the beautiful amoria volutes, and even in the cooler waters of the southern part of that continent, such uniquely patterned shells as **Gunther's Volute** exist. (*Paramoria guntheri* (E.A. Smith, 1886). 1.5 in./4cm)

From deeply set lobster traps in the cold waters of southern Australia come this spiny **Flinder's Vase,** a collector's item reaching a length of 8 inches (20cm). (*Altivasum flindersi* (Verco, 1914)).

OPPOSITE: The Great Ocean Road running along the cool ocean waters in the State of Victoria, Australia is an easy access to beach collecting and reef exploration.

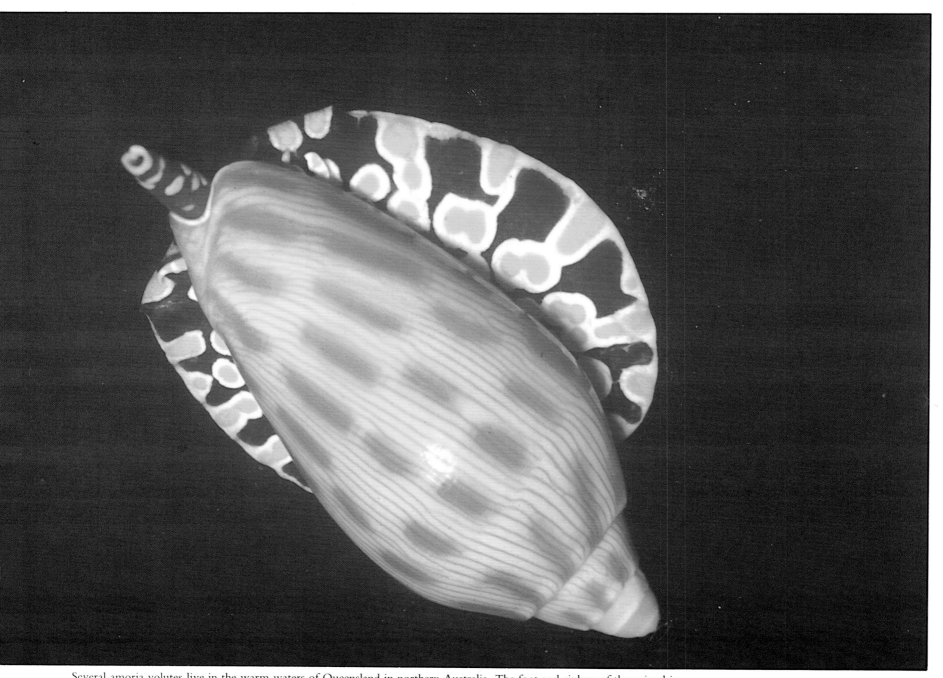

Several amoria volutes live in the warm waters of Queensland in northern Australia. The foot and siphon of the animal is sometimes as beautiful as the shell, as in this **Elliot's Volute.** (*Amoria ellioti* (Sowerby, 1864). 3.5 in./9cm)

Becoming scarcer because of over-collecting by Asian trawlers, the famous **Bedall's Volute** was discovered in 1878 off the Northern Territory of Australia. Its unique pattern is reminiscent of Australian Aborigine art. (*Volutoconus bednalli* (Brazier, 1878). 4 in./10cm)

The edges of this 2-inch **Girgyllus Star-shell** from the Southwest Pacific bear two rows of exquisitely sculptured spines, no doubt a protection against being swallowed by hungry fish. (*Bolma girgyllus* (Reeve, 1861). 2 in./5cm)

Among the Melanesian Islands of the southwestern Pacific, such as New Guinea and the Solomon Islands, shells are particularly colorful. Here on the horizon, just to the northwest of Guadacanal Island in the Solomons, is Savo Island of Bali-Hai charm. Among the wrecks from World War II sea battles lie gorgeous shells, including Star-shells, showy scallops and the White-spotted Cowrie (p. 128).

Many of the hundred kinds of scallops are not edible, but some are the object of admiration and wonderment by avid shell collectors. This beautiful specimen is from the tropical Pacific. (*Aequipecten* species. 3 in./8cm)

Almost every pastel hue is displayed by this common sand-dwelling **Australian Cardita** clam. Similar, although not as colorful, species live in southeastern United States and the Pacific side of central America. (*Cardita crassicosta* (Lamarck, 1819). 2 in./5cm)

Typical of northern Australia and neighboring New Guinea is the massive foot-long **Heavy Baler,** used by the Australian Aborigines to bale out leaking canoes. The living animal may weigh over 20 pounds. (*Melo umbilicata* Sowerby, 1826. 30cm)

Despite their large size and light weight, the shell of the **Tessellate Tun** is surprisingly strong. The soft-bodied animal is huge and glides rapidly over sandy bottoms in search of starfish and sea cucumbers. (*Tonna tessellata* (Lamarck, 1822). 4 in./10cm)

The **Precious Wentletrap** was so rare and sought after so much during the eighteenth century, that it was reported that clever Oriental dealers fashioned rice-paste counterfeits. The species is fairly common in Queensland, Australia. *Epitonium scalare* (Linnaeus, 1758). 2.5 in./6cm)

Hallmark of the marine intertidal ledges along the shores of northwest Australia is the **Monodon Murex** with its very long, recurved spines. It preys on oysters. (*Chicoreus cornucervi* (Röding, 1798). 4 in./10cm)

The beautiful glossy surface of this **Golden-brown Ancilla** snail from eastern Australis is kept in pristine condition by the soft fleshy mantle and foot of the animal. (*Ancillista velesiana* Iredale, 1936. 2.5 in./6cm)

Lizard Island, shown here, and other offshore Queensland islands near the Great Australian Barrier Reef are now nature sanctuaries where shell and coral collecting is forbidden. Larval forms from these safe breeding populations float many miles to distant shores and keep nature's stock plentiful elsewhere for collectors.

The **Channeled Volute** owes its name to the minute furrow separating the whorls in the spire of the shell. The uncommon Queensland sand-dweller has five spiral rows of curved dots. None of the *Amoria* volutes have an operculum. (*Amoria canaliculata* (McCoy, 1869). 2 in./5cm)

Related to the giant *Tridacna* clams (p. 93), the **Bear Paw Clam** also lives exposed on the surface of flat reefs of the southwest Pacific. They are popular ornamental shells used as bowls. (*Hippopus hippopus* (Linnaeus, 1758) 8 in./20cm)

SOUTHWEST
PACIFIC

No area of the world is as rich in shells as the Philippine Archipelago with its hundreds of ocean-bounded islands. The warm waters and rich, protected inland seas and bays are ideal for the growth of thousands of kinds of seashells. In the early 1800's the famous shell collector Hugh Cuming discovered more than a thousand new species of marine and land-dwelling shells.

The tropical southwest Pacific harbors several species of delphinula turbans recognized by their operculum, or trapdoor, which is circular horny and festooned with hairlike bristles. The **Imperial Delphinula** was discovered in the Philippines in 1840. (*Angaria delphinus* (Linnaeus, 1758), form *melanacantha* (Reeve, 1842). 3 in./8cm)

Monofilament nets lowered to the sea bottom by Philippine fishermen have been bringing up many new species in recent years, such as this **Victor Dan's Delphinula** described by a Japanese conchologist in 1980. (*Angaria vicdani* Kosuge, 1980 2 in./5cm)

Once considered very rare, **Martin's Tibia** was first discovered in 1877, but remained an elusive collector's item until Philippine shell collectors learned how to sample the sea bottom where this still uncommon shell lives. Compare with the commoner Spindle Tibia on page 146. (*Tibia martinii* (Marrat, 1877). 5 in./12cm)

The soft animal of the common **Major Harp** produces the shell of this glossy, delicately patterned sand-dweller. It feeds on crabs by covering its victim in a ball of sticky mucus and sand. (*Harpa major* Röding, 1798. 3.5 in./9cm)

Producing a forest of prickly spines is a miracle of creation best exemplified by the **Venus Comb Murex.** Tiny extensions of the fleshy mantle exude liquid lime, which then crystalizes into stiff rods. (*Murex pecten* Lightfoot, 1786. Philippines. 4.5 in./11cm)

Cowries add glossy shelly material and pigments to the outer surface of their shells by extending the mantle, with its lime-giving glands, over the outside. The extensions on this **Tiger Cowrie** mantle are sensory feelers. (*Cypraea tigris* Linnaeus, 1758. Indo-Pacific. 4 in./10cm)

This eastern Asian Murex has a southern Philippine subspecies named the **Miyoko Murex.** It is brought up from deep water attached to monofilament fish nets. (*Pterynotus loebbeckei* subspecies *miyokoae* Kosuge, 1979. 2.5 in./6cm)

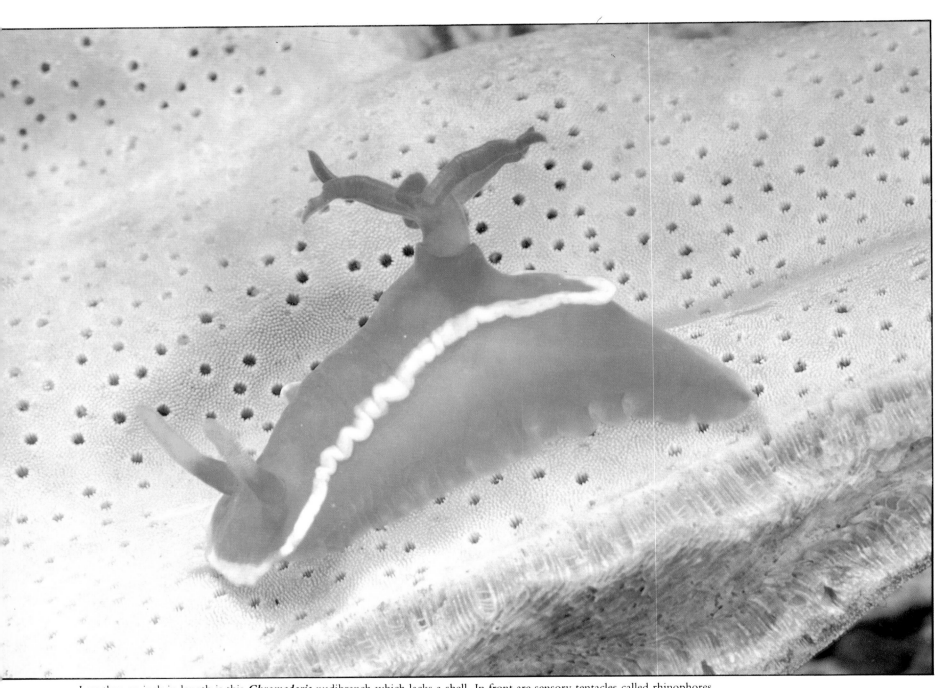

Less than an inch in length is this **Chromodoris** nudibranch which lacks a shell. In front are sensory tentacles called rhinophores. On the back is a clump of gills for extracting oxygen from the water. This is a widely distributed Indo-Pacific nudibranch that feeds on bryozoans. (*Chromodoris species.* 2cm)

The venus clams prefer to dig down into a sandy bottom. Ridges and raised lines help keep them wedged down. In some species, the ridges are lost and replaced by color stripes and tentlike markings, as in the case of the **Camp Pitar Venu** from the Indo-Pacific. (*Lioconcha castrensis* (Linnaeus, 1758) 2 in./5cm)

Once bringing over a thousand dollars at public shell auctions, the **White-spotted Cowrie** of the southwestern Pacific has been discovered in moderate numbers in the Solomons and northeastern Australia. (*Cypraea guttata* Gmelin, 1791. 1.5 in./4cm)

Still the shell collector's dream-desire is the richly colored **Golden Cowrie,** a prize shell once worn around the neck only of Fijian chiefs. Scuba divers have found many sponge-encrusted caves where this species lives, particularly in Samar Island, Philippines, (*Cypraea aurantia* Gmelin, 1791. 3.5 in./9cm)

The **Princely Volute** from the southern Philippines was once a much sought-after species. The first ones found in 1825 were the rare red form, but later a number of yellow and brown forms began arriving in European shell markets to start prices tumbling. (*Cymbiola aulica* (Sowerby, 1825) 4 in./10cm)

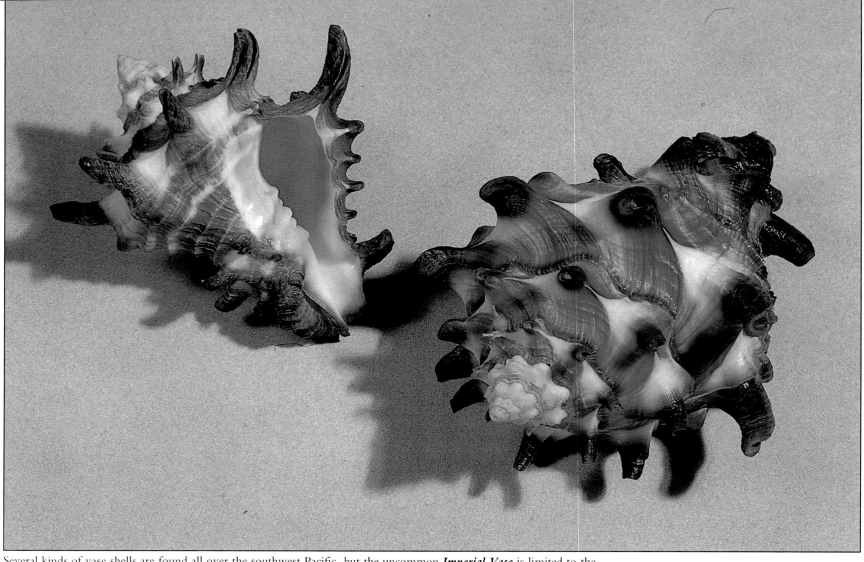

Several kinds of vase shells are found all over the southwest Pacific, but the uncommon **Imperial Vase** is limited to the central Philippines. (*Vasum tubiferum* (Anton, 1839). 3 in./7.5cm)

This is the true **Loebbecke's Murex** originally found in southern China about 1878. It comes in white, peach and lavender colors and is wider than its Philippine subspecies *miyokae* seen on page 125. (*Pterynotus loebbeckei* (Kobelt, 1879) 2 in./5cm)

Found offshore in quiet Philippine waters is this 2-inch (5 cm) **Kiener's Delphinula**. The operculum is thin, circular and horny in texture. (*Angaria sphaerula* (Kiener, 1839))

Renowned for its intricate spines and beaded surface, the **Giryllus star-shell** is rarely brought up in dredges by fishermen in the northern Philippines and off Taiwan. (*Bolma girgyllus* (Reeve, 1861). 2 in./5cm)

Saul's Murex was named in 1841 after a wealthy Englishman whose wife was an ardent shell collector. It differs from the similar Rose-branch Murex (p. 99) in having a white inner lip which lacks tiny brown pimples. Moderately common offshore in the East Indies (*Chicoreus saulii* (Sowerby, 1841) 4 in./10cm)

Cut across with a diamond saw, this **Chambered Nautilus** displays the internal chambers once filled with gas. The shell inspired Oliver Wendell Holmes to write his poem "The Chambered Nautilus": "Build thee more stately mansions . . . ." (*Nautilus pompilius* Linnaeus, 1758. Philippines. 6 in./15cm)

FOLLOWING PAGE: An array of turban shells (*Turbo* spp.).

JAPAN

Japan is a shell-conscious country. The late Emperor Hirohito was a marine biologist and shell collector. Several shrines have been erected in honor of shells, including one that refers to the Mikomoto pearl-raising venture. Shells are abundant from the cold waters of northern Hokkaido to the quiet waters of the Inland Sea to the tropical waters of Kyushu and Okinawa. Many abalones and colorful scallops are maricultured in special tanks for food purposes.

Cleanest and most graceful of the Japanese murexes is the pure-white, frilly **Alabaster Murex,** a deep-water collector's item ranging from southern Japan to the Philippines. (*Siratus alabaster* (Reeve, 1845) 5 in./12cm)

Not a true murex, but certainly resembling one, is **Burnett's Murex**, which has a strong spine at the base of the lip with which it opens oysters. It is common offshore in Korea and northern Japan. (*Ceratostoma burnetti* (Adams and Reeve, 1859) 4 in./10cm)

The **Peri Japelion** whelk from the cold waters off Hokkaido, northern Japan, has a charming coiling ramp at the top of each whorl, but has the dull-brown finish of so many Arctic species. (*Japelion pericochlion* (Schrenck, 1862) 4 in./10cm)

Similar in meat quality to the Hardshell Clam, the **Reddish Callista** has a very attractive, rayed shell but is not abundant enough to be commercially important. It ranges from the Philippines and Taiwan north to southern Japan. (*Callista erycina* (Linnaeus, 1758) 3 in./8cm)

Japan is the land of Latiaxis shells, a particularly spinose and strangely shaped, murexlike group of deep-water snails. They are very variable and bear many names, but perhaps the commonest is the **Pagoda Latiaxis** and its **Spinose** form shown here. (*Latiaxis pagodus* form *spinosa* Hirase, 1908. 1 in./2.5cm)

The strange, flattened, somewhat detached whorls of **Mawe's Latiaxis** have made it a popular novelty in shell collections for 150 years. It was named after Mrs. John Mawe, a London shell dealer in the 1830's. (*Latiaxis mawae* (Griffith and Pidgeon, 1834) Japan. 2 in./5cm)

The bonnet shells are usually tropical inhabitants, but the **Striped Bonnet** loves the cold waters of Taiwan and northern China. It lives in water from 10 to 300 feet deep and feeds on sea biscuits. (*Phalium flammiferum* (Röding, 1798) 3.5 in./9cm)

Largest of the rare Slit Shells is **Rumphius's Slit Shell** originally dredged in deep water in Indonesia in 1877. Many more specimens including one 12 inches (30cm) across have been recently trawled from off Taiwan and southern Japan. A large one is worth several thousand dollars (*Pleurotormaria rumphii* Schepman, 1879. 10 in./25cm)

From Natal, South Africa, to Japan the deep-sea fauna has a common history—a deep, cold, dark marine corridor that connects the shells from these distant points. Here is the rare Japanese **Teramachi Slit Shell**, a subspecies of the African Slit Shell, seen on page 85. (*Pleurotormaria africana* subspecies *teramachii* Kuroda, 1955. 5 in./12cm)

Resembling a pagoda, the **Japanese Wonder Shell** could inspire any architect with its Frank Lloyd Wright-style ramp on its shoulder. This 3-inch, deep-sea species is unique among the turrid snails. (*Thatcheria mirabilis* Angas, 1877. 8cm)

The list of known Slit Shells gradually grows as new collecting methods are developed and as new oceanic habitats are explored. Since the first species was discovered in 1856, there has been a new one found on an average of every eight years, the most recent being **Victor Dan's Slit Shell** from the Philippines. (*Pleurotormaria vicadani* Kosuge, 1980. 3 in./8cm)

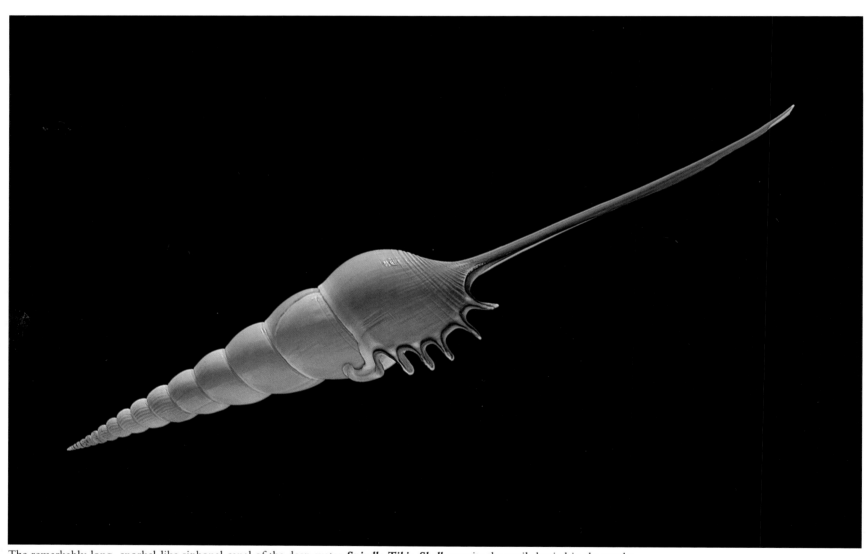

The remarkably long, snorkel-like siphonal canal of the deep-water **Spindle Tibia Shell** permits the snail, buried in the sandy mud bottom, to draw in fresh seawater to breathe. The shell is common in parts of the Philippines but difficult to collect unbroken. (*Tibia fusus* (Linnaeus, 1758) 9 in./ 23cm)

Dubbed the "original shell collectors," the group of worldwide carrier-shells have an instinct to seek out and attach foreign bodies, including shells, coral bits and stones to itself. Sometimes a beautiful colony of bryozoans will form on the outside of the **Pallid Carrier-shell.** *(Xenophora pallidula* (Reeve, 1842) 3 in./8cm)

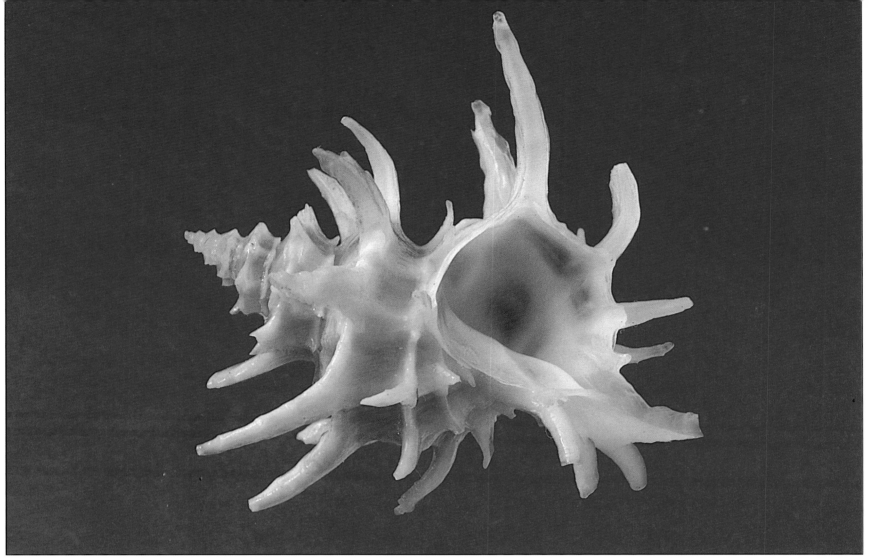

The true **Pagoda Latiaxis** from the offshore waters of Japan is not as spinose, nor is its spire as high, as its subspecies the Spinose Latiaxis, seen on page 140. (*Latiaxis pagodus* (A Adams, 1852) 1 in./2.5cm)

Somewhat resembling its cousin, the New England Neptune, seen on page 43, the 4-inch **Grammatus Whelk** from the cold waters of Japan also has strong, square spiral cords. It is normally covered with a brown outer skin, or periostracum. (*Ancistrolepis grammatus* (Dall, 1907). 10cm)

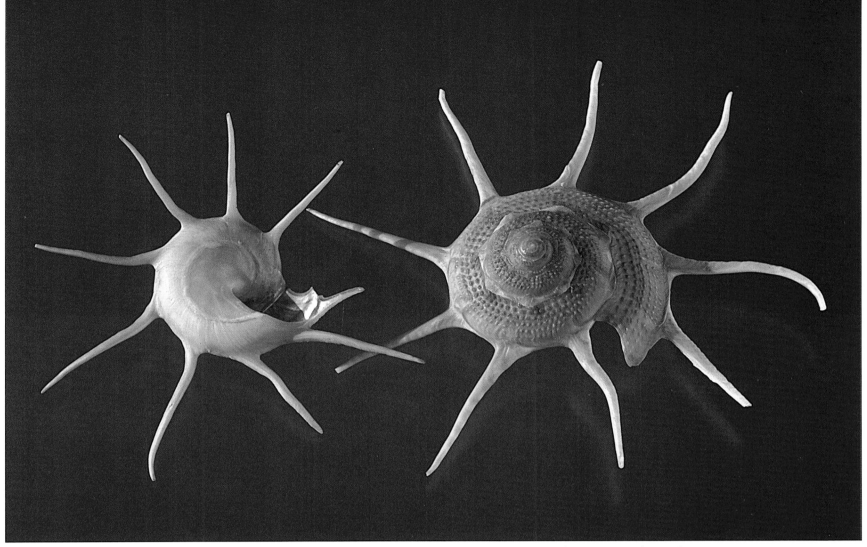

Typical of many deep-water Japanese shells is the common long-spined **Yoka Star Turban.** Like its spineless turban cousins, it has a white, smooth shelly trapdoor, or operculum. (*Guildfordia yoka* (Jousseaume, 1888) 3 in./8cm)

Discovered in 1872 in Mauritius, **Du Savel's Cone** remained a unique mystery until specimens began appearing in Okinawan waters. Soon after, scuba divers began recovering a few more of these rare shells in Philippine waters. (*Conus dusaveli* (H. Adams, 1872) 2 in./5cm)

FOLLOWING PAGE: A potpourri of gastropod snails.

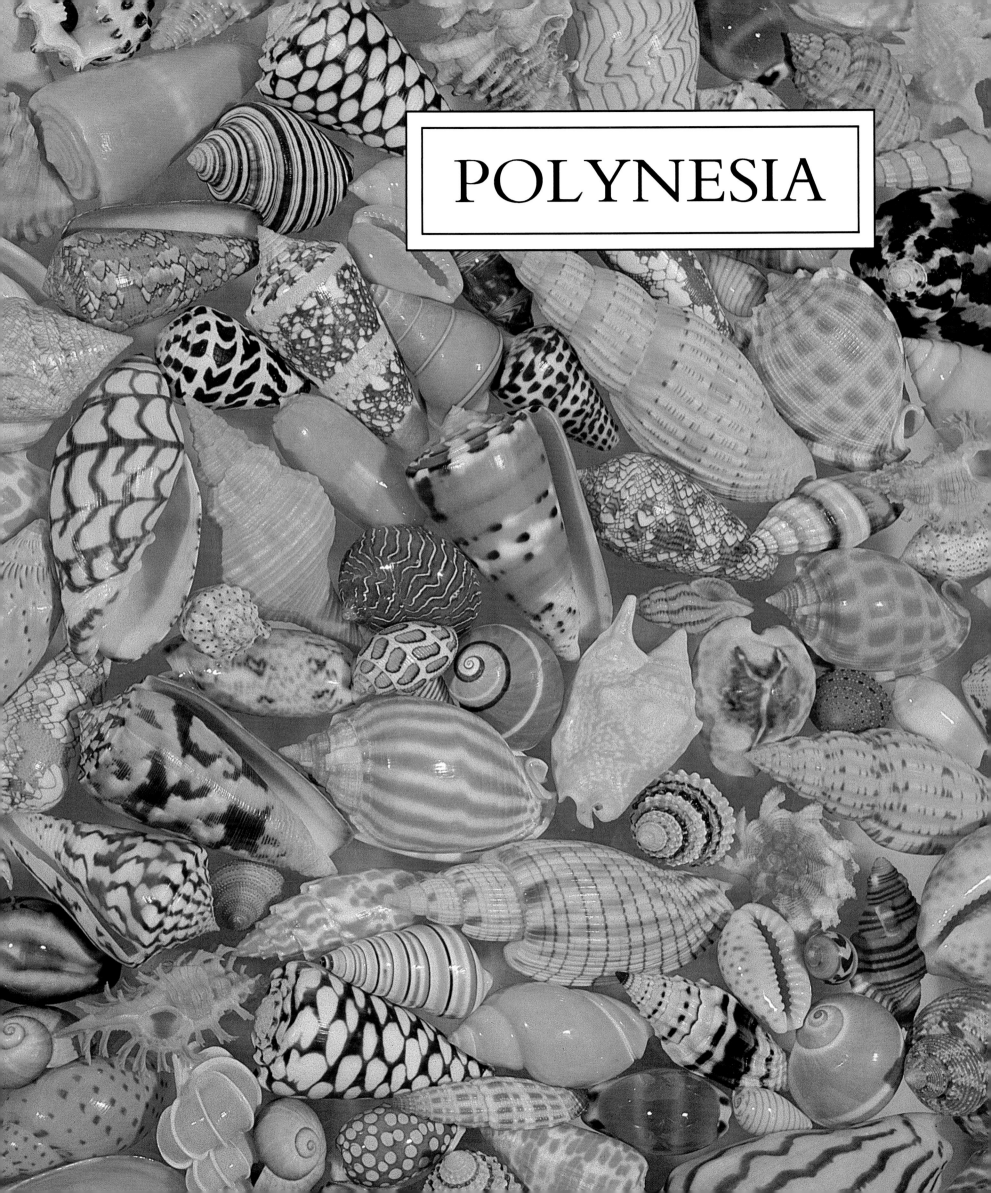

POLYNESIA

The animals of these Hawaiian specimens of Harp shells are as exquisite as the shells. The end of the foot can be voluntarily dropped off in the fashion of some chameleons. Larger shells are the **Major Harp** (*Harpa major* Röding, 1798. 3 in./8cm); the smaller are the **Minor Harp** (*Harpa amouretta* Röding, 1798. 2 in./5cm)

OPPOSITE: Polynesia with its many small isolated islands and lagoons, such as Bora Bora in French Polynesia, have beckoned shell collectors since the time of La Perouse, Captain Cook and Captain Bligh. Although not as rich in species, these coral-bordered volcanic islands have their own distinctive shell fauna.

Of the dozen species of Spider conchs, only half are present in Polynesia. Among the common, more colorful species is the **Orange Spider Conch**, not infrequently found in shallow water near algae beds and sand bottoms. (*Lambis crocata* (Link, 1807) 4.5 in./11cm)

The rocky shores of Polynesia are blessed with an abundance of common drupe snails, including the violet–mouthed **Purple Pacific Drupe (***Drupa Morum*** (Röding, 1798). 1 in./2.5cm) and the orange–mouthed **Digitate Pacific Drupe (***Drupa grossularia*** (Röding, 1798). 1 in./2.5cm)

FOLLOWING PAGE: Armchair shell collectors long to visit Bora Bora in the Society Islands of Polynesia.

BIBLIOGRAPHY AND INDICES

The literature on shells is very extensive. Over 3,000 popular and scientific articles are written on the subject each year, and there are about a hundred major books in print that deal with the biology or identification of mollusks. An annual listing is published in volume 9 of the *Zoological Record,* BIOSIS, Philadelphia.

INTRODUCTORY BOOKS

Abbott, R. Tucker. 1982. *Kingdom of the Seashell.* New York: Bonanza Books.
Emerson, William K., and Andreas Feininger. 1972. *Shells.* New York: Viking Press.
Hoyt, Murray. 1967. *Jewels from the Ocean Deep.* New York: G.P. Putnam's Sons.
Jacobson, Morris K., and William Emerson. 1971. *Wonders of the World of Shells.* New York: Dodd, Mead.
Johnstone, Kathleen Y. 1957. *Sea Treasures: A Guide to Shell Collecting.* Boston: Houghton Mifflin.
————. 1970. *Collecting Seashells.* New York: Grosset & Dunlap.
Rogers, Julia E. [1908] 1960. *The Shell Book.* Reprint, up-dated by Harald A. Rehder. Boston: Charles T. Branford, Co.
Stix, Hugh, Marguerite Stix, and R. Tucker Abbott. 1968. *The Shell: Five Hundred Million Years of Inspired Design.* New York: Harry N. Abrams.

ADVANCED TEXTBOOKS

Hyman, Libbie H. 1967. *The Invertebrates. Mollusca I.* Vol. 6. New York: McGraw-Hill.
Malek, Emile A., and Thomas C. Chang. 1974. *Medical and Economic Malacology.* New York: Academic Press.
Purchon, R. D. 1968. *The Biology of the Mollusca.* Oxford: Oxford University Press.
Solem, Alan. 1974. *The Shell Makers.* New York: John Wiley and Sons.
Vaught, Kay C. 1989. *A Classification of the Living Mollusca.* Melbourne, Fla.: American Malacologists.
Wilbur, Karl M., ed. 1982-1984. *The Mollusca.* Vols. 1-7. Orlando, Fla.: Academic Press
Yonge, C. M., and T. E. Thompson. 1976. *Living Marine Molluscs.* London: Collins and Sons.

IDENTIFICATION GUIDES

Abbott, R. Tucker. 1985. *Sea Shells of the World.* rev. ed. New York: Golden Nature Guide, Golden Press.
————. 1989. *Compendium of Landshells.* Melbourne, Fla.: American Malacologists.
————. 1974. *American Seashells.* 2nd ed. New York: Van Nostrand/Reinhold.
————. 1986. *Seashells of North America.* 2nd ed. New York: Golden Field Guide, Golden Press.
Abbott, R. Tucker, and S. Peter Dance. *Compendium of Seashells.* Melbourne, Fla.: American Malacologists.
Cernohorsky, Walter O. 1967; 1972. *Marine Shells of the Pacific.* Vols. 1 and 2. Sydney: Pacific Publications.
Dance, S. Peter. 1974. *The Collector's Encyclopedia of Seashells.* New York: McGraw-Hill.
Eisenberg, Jerome M. 1981. *A Collector's Guide to Seashells of the World.* New York: McGraw-Hill.
Kay, E. Alison. 1971. *Hawaiian Marine Shells.* Honolulu: Bishop Museum Press.
Keen, A. Myra. 1971. *Sea Shells of Tropical West America.* 2nd. ed. Stanford: Standford University Press.
Powell, A. W. Baden. 1979. *New Zealand Mollusca.* Auckland and London: Collins.

Rios, E. C. 1985. *Seashells of Brazil.* Rio Grande, Brazil: Museu Oceanografico.
Sharabati, Doreen. 1984. *Red Sea Shells.* London: Routledge & Kegan Paul.
Springsteen, F. J., and F. M. Leobrera. 1986. *Shells of the Philippines.* Manila: Carfel Seashell Museum.
Sutty, Lesley. 1986. *Seashell Treasures of the Caribbean.* New York: E. P. Dutton.
Warmke, Germaine and R. Tucker Abbott. 1975. *Caribbean Seashells.* New York: Dover Publications.

SPECIAL FAMILIES

Bratcher, Twila, and Walter O. Cernohorsky. 1987. *Living Terebras of the World.* Melbourne, Fla. American Malacologists.
Burgess, C. M. 1985. *Cowries of the World.* Orlando, Fla.: Gordon Verhoef, Seacomber Publications.
Lamprell, Kevin. 1986. *Spondylus, Spiny Oysters of the World.* Bathurst, Australia: Robert Brown & Associates.
Lane, Frank W. *Kingdom of the Octopus.* 1957. New York: Sheridan House.
Walls, Jerry G. 1979. *Cone Shells: A Synopsis of the Living Conidae.* Neptune City, N.J.: T.F.H. Publications.
Ward, Peter Douglas. 1988. *In Search of the Nautilus.* New York: Simon and Schuster.
Weaver, Clifton S., and John E. du Pont. 1970. *The Living Volutes.* Greenville, Del.: Delaware Museum of Natural History.

ART, HISTORY AND LITERATURE

Conklin, William A. 1985. *Nature's Art: The Inner and Outer Dimensions of the Shell.* Columbia: University South Carolina Press.
Cox, Ian. 1957. *The Scallop.* London: Shell Transport and Trading Co.
Dance, S. Peter. 1969. Berkeley: *Rare Shells.* University of California Press.
————. 1986. *A History of Shell Collecting.* Leiden: E. J. Brill.
Hogendorn, Jan, and Marion Johnson. 1986. *The Shell Money of the Slave Trade.* Cambridge: Cambridge University Press. Krauss, Helen K. 1965. Shell Art. New York: Hearthside Press.
Reece, Norine C. 1958. *The Cultured Pearl—Jewel of Japan.* Rutland, Vt.: Charles E. Tuttle.
Ritchie, Carson I. A. 1974. *Shell Carving—History and Techniques.* New Brunswick, N.J. A. S. Barnes.
Saul, Mary, 1974. *Shells—An Illustrated Guide to a Timeless and Fascinating World.* New York: Doubleday.
Shirai, Shohei. 1970. *The Story of Pearls.* San Francisco: Japan Publishing Trading Co.
Travers, Louise A. 1962. *The Romance of Shells in Nature and Art.* New York: M. Barrows.

SHELL MAGAZINES AND DIRECTORIES

American Conchologist. A quarterly published by the Conchologists of America. Lynn Scheu, ed. 1222 Holsworth Lane, Louisville, KY 40222.
Hawaiian Shell News. Published by the Hawaiian Malacological Society. P.O. Box 22130, Honolulu, HI 96815.
Of Sea and Shore. Tom Rice, ed. Privately published (revised 1990). P.O. Box 219, Port Gamble, WA 98364.
Register of American Malacologists. 1987. A "Who's Who" listing of 1,200 conchologists. American Malacologists, Melbourne, Fl.
Say It Right! 1987. (35 mm.) Stereo tape on how to pronounce the scientific names of seashells of North America. American Malacologists, Melbourne, Fl.
A Sheller's Directory of Clubs, Books, Periodicals and Dealers. 13th ed. 1989. Tom Rice, ed. Privately published. P.O. Box 219, Port Gamble, WA 98364